Seatonian Exercises
and Other Verses

Seatonian Exercises

and Other Verses

DEREK BREWER

UNICORN PRESS

LONDON

For Elisabeth, family and friends

Unicorn Press
21 Afghan Road
London SW11 2QD

email unicorn@tradford.demon.co.uk
website www.boydell.co.uk

First published by Unicorn Press 2000

Typeset by Ferdinand Pageworks, London
Printed in Great Britain by Cambridge University Press

ISBN 0 906 29061 9

CONTENTS

Introduction

The poems gathered here are a series of reflections on a life-time's observation of war, love, integrity in suffering, and the problems of faith. They vary from complex speculations, allusive and mixed in nature, to shorter poems and brief notes on everyday experience. In addition there are sections on the medieval stories of Troilus and Criseyde and the Arthurian legend.

'Seatonian Exercises' are poems written for the annual competition set in the University of Cambridge for 'a poem on a sacred subject' which have wide references, and are speculative rather than devotional. They are submitted anonymously, with identifying mottos, retained here.

An asterisk * beside the date at the end denotes award of the prize.

The author wishes to thank the Master and Fellows of Emmanuel College for assistance in preparing the typescript for publication.

God has no
favourites

EPIPHANY

I

Twelfth Night 1945, or What you Will

A night for drama and for festival.
We put up a good show towards the enemy,
In rain and darkness acting unlearned parts
In crazy scenery of unseen mountain chaos,
The limelight, short dull glares of Verey lights,
As red as blood, as shadowy as truth;
And Spandaus make a stuttering commentary.
And this our playhouse is our sulphurous Hell.
Applause is given by the great guns clap.
Explosions flash, the guns now shout,   10
We struggle up a narrow winding path
To some great hill, which may for us be truth,
And search, and faith, although we bring no gold,
No sweetness, no precious ointment for a wound,
But only steel and bitter smoke and dark.
Our light is artificial moonlight, suiting
Well inverted day. Far back our searchlight beams
Bounce off the clouds that cut off heaven from us.
We labour still in mud upon a hill
Which is our only solid certainty.   20

No babe up there. The stable ruined.
When we arrive, in that stone manger
No babe, but I will sleep: the animals,
The mother, all gone, gone, dissolved in mud.
Under a roof as holy and as holed
As one of Botticelli's. We'll take the family's
Place and try to keep our powder dry. The grain
All spilt; the tired soldiers loll like those
Who slept before the Resurrection, one or two
Flat out, others whimpering and another   30
Springing up with ignorant mad anxiety.
But that's to come, we're not at heaven's gate yet.
We soldier on, no kings; gentiles in every sense,
Though not gentle. The star cannot be seen.
The resurrection is a long way off.
We keep the narrow way, thigh-deep in mud,
Because on either side are minefields where
Corpses are most effective signs, preserving
Life. And trapped within our track the mule
Who did not choose this life to share our war,   40
Infertile hybrid, slowly drowns in mud.
My pistol's bullet ends his misery as
A German's would mine. Then would my playing cease.
This dark mirror shattered, would all then be clear?
Epiphany of heaven rise out of mud?
That blazing timeless true and truthful light,
Once glowing in a child within world's dark,
Would I then be a part of? Yet I still
With fear evade. The darkness punctuated
By a spark, with light uncertain of the minds   50
Of wavering men, seems still a preferable text,

2

For me to find a cue, and clue. I want
The showing. Is this your will, your peace?

II

And Private Salmon lost his trousers
And his boots in mud, sucked off, obscene.
There was no epiphanic show, and mud
Could only re-inforce his privacy,
And three days later, unrevealed, he joined
The larger army made of mud, and in   60
A flash all was for ever known or lost.

III

Shock-shell

Immediate as whine, shriek, crash, the upsurge
Of earth hurled, burnt, all in a moment's flame,
Makes us dive, sweating, rabbits wishing we
Had burrows; and death intensifies
The will to live. In the after-second's
Retrospect we know our life was then,
When least we knew, and most intensely lived.

IV

The self-creating moment justifies
By vividness all further time in life,   70
Piercing the tedious crawl towards the grave.
It stabs us through to fix us to the earth,
A little death, a timeless spurt of life,

A seed, whose instant flower bursts like a shell,[1]
White sky-puff in the heavenly blue, while we
Cower, generating painful unknown life.

The scene is the mountains of the so-called Gothic Line, Italy. Artificial moonlight was created by directing searchlights on to the clouds some ten miles behind the front line. Verey lights were flares shot from a pistol to give a brief illumination. Spandaus were German machine-guns. Epiphany is a kind of revelation. References are made to Donne, St Paul and the first chapter of St John's Gospel.

* 1983

---

1 Airbursts, shells which explode high in the air to disseminate shrapnel.

ANOTHER EPIPHANY

VENUS RISING FROM THE SEA (VENUS ANADYOMENE)

*One ancient story of the birth of Venus is that she rose fully formed from
the sea born of the genitals of Saturn castrated by his son Jove. Botticelli's
picture is the most beautiful image of her first appearance.*

I

You rise up from the fecund infinite sea
Engendered from the bloody sperm of male
Desires; yet less than masculine, more strong
In quintessential female power one could
Not think nor hope. Not virginal, yet still
Unknown; carried to us on the breath
Of childish sighs, pregnant with all our fantasies
Of love and fruit, floating free in modest
Nakedness, a light to lighten daylight,
A beauty born of pain and terror, loss,
Who promises no less, and whom we need,
The impossible she, whose image shows her absence,
To recognise which makes our acting necessary
And by acceptance of our emptiness
Keeps space to fill with possibility.

II

And those fisher-boys, almost men,
As they drag out, plunge in the warm sea –
Well might their hot fancies see in the foam,

The naked women of their dreams emerge,
Against blue sky, in spume and splash,
Born of sperm and blood, coming ashore.
To bring love, floating on magic shell.
The waves break and are lost in a frenzy
Of whitened foam among the rocks, sink in sand.
The dream dissolves. The waves return,
As in remotest time some creature
Swam from the warm sea, and stayed, and became woman.
Still our blood carries the salt of those ancient waters
And still our fantasies welcome incoming love,
Which does not always sink into the sand
But stays, leaves coloured shells in which we hear
The everlasting murmured promise
Of the living, salt-bitter sea.

EVOLUTION PRODUCES
THE SHOPGIRL

Out of a warm sea once you crawled –
Doesn't it still run warm in your heart?
In muddy forests your child clung to your hairy sides.
Yet here you sit with thin fingers
Twiddling papers,
Air-conditioned virgin,
And keep your head down.
– You look up now at me, and quickly away.
My thought's misinterpreted,
But not misunderstood.
Is evolution thus fulfilled?

THE HAPPY LAND

There is an Old English poem on this subject, based on a fourth-century Latin poem by Lactantius. It describes the Earthly Paradise, as do, in another way, the medieval poems on 'The Land of Cockayne', and the modern American folk-song 'The Big Rock Candy Mountain'.

In that land shall be no committees
Nor arrangements to be made for anyone
But all will work well from good will,
Honest men knowing what best is.

There shall be no examinations, pending
The ultimate judgment, which all will pass;
There will be just a little work, to make
Leisure attractive and sleep refreshing.

We shall all be young but not absurdly so,
The girls friendly with good figures and
Excellent conversation; the men
Eager not aggressive, interested and fit.

The weather will alternate as in England
But with rather more sunshine and snow;
No building later than nineteen thirty
Shall survive, but all shall have central heating.

There shall be mountains where one is quite alone
Yet find a refuge at night-fall; forests; and fields

With hedgerows; lonely rocky coasts;
Colleges with lawns and flower beds; churches
　　without pews.

There shall be little noise, except bird and beast
(Who will require little attention because we
Shall all help) and musical instruments and choirs;
No radio, television, aeroplanes or cars.

Sailing-boats, steam engines and horses there will be
But no metalled roads; medicine and science
But no industry; books, no newspapers;
Gossip, no news; games, no wars.

When the Queen comes we shall honour her
Without crowding; report our activities
And show her our paintings, which no doubt
Will be full of horrors and obscenities unmentionable.

*'Filius orientis est Lucifer': the East
is one of the Devil's names*

EX ORIENTE LUX

I

ON THE BREAKING UP OF A NATION

Who comes leaping over the eastern hill
With spears of light to nail our dull
Quiescence, to prise away warm hands, kill
Our loves, empty us of desire, once so full?

The high grasses greenly envy the blue sky.
Sleepers awake to moan the grimy morn.
Mourners raise up their poppy-scarlet cry.
From the ruins of our sins the black cover's drawn.

Your hot foot treads us to coals; we burn;
The greasy smoke bleeds over factory-farms.   10
Hatred and agony grind the earth red; we turn
To tear each other, cursing with psalms.

What forced enmity of love d'you bring? Light wakes
To hellish love. But Lucifer-Venus fades soon.
Then bells boom bullets; cross or crescent shakes.
Our hope, Venus-Lucifer returning under the mad
   fertile moon.

Her light will make darkness visible. Then
We will melt into house field mountain, all will freeze
In stony air. Virgins will scream. Let men
Kill, kill, till pain cease in death. We find dark ease.   20

II

Egyptian Prayer

Praise to you, Ra, light god, life god
Surging in your boat from the dark waves of night.
Hail to you, Ra, perfection of each day,
All eyes see you and by you,
Their light goes out when you sail down the sky
And darkness brings nothingness.
You stir us at dawn,
Your brightness opens the eyes of the flock,
The bullocks pull carts for you, men sweat,
The girls walk with swaying hips and large dark eyes,   30
In the muddy river women wash to the whiteness
    of dawn,
The waterwheels pour forth their benison,
The green fields rejoice, children shout at play
The brown clay grows on the wheel, caressed by the
    potter's hand.
Then you sail in redness beyond the dry mountains
And the colours die and all sleep as dead.

III

THE EGYPTIAN WIFE'S LAMENT

The East is paler, light returns, Ra comes,
But not for me, and he has taken you,
The dawn wind chills.
No light comes to you my beloved.   40
Never again your sun rises to me.
Your dark hair shone like sun on your head to me,
Your face rayed gladness,
You were my sun, you pierced me with your warmth.
Never again will you come as the light comes
To lighten my darkness with your bright strength.
The light comes from the East
Never again to warm the cold stone of my heart.
You have gone down in blood in the western sky,
You have sailed for ever to circle heaven   50
Never again to land upon me.
Your going has taken the light of my life.
Let me follow you soon, my life, my beloved,
Let me take the dark boat with black sail,
Follow the sun's boat round the earth,
But join you in darkness for ever, my beloved.

IV

The Defeated
An episode in the Civil War

At dawn they left their broken comrades and the
   unburied dead,
The walls collapsing; they hungry, thirsting, but
Full of righteousness; bravely upright they marched,
Marching westward, pursued by light to seek the dark, 60
Carrying their swords unsheathed, drums beating,
   flying flags,
Their hopes behind, in front the glory of hopeless war,
And more defeat, but their flags flying, honour saved
   to thud of drum,
Monotonous repeat, obstinate iteration
Of unbroken will. To be weak is the only misery,
Only wickedness. Surrender is not despair,
Nor need despair be surrender's cause.
So swagger on, observe the protocols,
Preserve some rag of self-regard,
The necessary human rite of human rights.   70
Pretend that in the end all will be well,
Retain the show, the chosen role, supreme
In will and virtue over natural decay,
And keep on marching, for west leads to east
And in the end defeat and victory are one
Under the clouds, the shining stars, the coursing sun.

V

EASTER SUNDAY AT THE GRAND CANYON

The East pales purely over our silence,
Stabs into our dim anticipation
Rimmed round the abyss, the reflected mountain,
From whence cometh no hope but what we pour in,   80
Into the depths, this Easter dawn, as we thinly wail
Our time-worn hymns, our banal modern words,
And shiver in the cold clear wind. Darkness
   driven back,
We see, layer upon coloured layer left
By the slow accretions of two billion years
Sliced like a cake by icy waters long since past,
Where desert followed sea and forest followed sand
To the most recent moment of recorded time,
To our brief second of the endless course,
Our thinnest layer of scum of cars and shacks,   90
Our shiny, tinny, poisonous scum, soon to be
– In geological time – covered yet again
In deadly dust, our hope for ages yet to come,
When later still more sea and forest, purer dirt,
Will hide our metalled tracks. So time itself will
Have forgotten us, sunk in the wasted West,
And our polluted vanity will drown
In mindless dust; the sun itself, now bright above
   the edge,
Will redden dully into nothingness,
Or explode in unimaginable cold.   100
And black for ever rule the coloured world.

But we for aeons will have met the dark,
Plunged through it into blinded light, escaped,
Whether we will or no, from ever-rolling tedious time
If the strange promise of this dawn holds good.

VI

Whitsunday Epiphany

In the grey dawn we walked westward along
The green lane, the flowers a blur, our sleepy eyes
Half open. On our backs, suddenly, a push
Of warmth, bright ray over the shoulder, then,
Awake, not looking back, we saw wild flowers,   110
Another chorus at dawn, of colour. We walked
And walked to double harmony until
We saw arise above the counterpointing leaves
Soft spires of bells which hung in clustered
Multicoloured white to red, beneath dark pines
That gently, greenly, sang to the blue sea wind.
The silent coloured chimes of those soft bells
So far beneath, upon our ground, still matched
The larger music of those sunlit heights.
All sang of life, a kind of eager joy,   120
Wordless, with tongues angelic, not of men.
We stopped, part of that music, beneath high trees
Through which we saw the infinite blue above.
We walked on westward through our lives,
To hear the far-off diapason of the sea,
The love-begetting, monster spewing sea;
Kept walking westward to our journey's end,

Sustained by that sweet music in our heads,
The languages not known but understood,
Transmitted by those strangely named bell-flowers.   130
The coloured music in the pines, foxgloves.

VII

I DREAMT SUCH A DREAM . . .

The light called me from sleep the very moment
Before the revelation came. Someone was going
To tell me something to my advantage,
To change my vision, understanding, life.
Was it some incandescent knowledge?
Some communication of the splendour,
The terrible beauty, of God? Or that
Someone loved me? Or that I loved someone?
The light came, I woke, and shall never know.   140

VIII

RESOLUTION

He springs up gallantly from the East
Masculine, phallic-rayed,
Puts (as was said) the stars to flight.
Well may they be dismayed,
Cold virgins of the dark, no feast
And no bridal morn, afraid.

Unfortunately this old cosmic fantasy seems

No longer to do. Let us try another.
Can we call the sun our mother?
Surely we feed on her beams?   150
Nor will this help. The bond is broken that bound us,
Women, animals and men, the earth and all in it
To sky and god and Heaven and Hell. Our minds
Must float from matter, irrecoverably alone,
For ever separate from meaningless dead matter.
Yet mind's matter too. Irretrievably part.
Why not take part, be taken apart,
To become a part, the keen self-knowing part,
Since matter matters too? So I will
Continue to be pleased to see the dawns of England's
   summer,   160
And welcome the day, even the grim evenings
Dark with cloud and the cold wind,
While I can still know them and know
Myself through them, and breathe the airs,
Sweet vernal airs, or the hot stink of petrol
And relish silence and restfulness
Like a sensible woman, and leave
The problem of God to sort Himself out
And me too, so that in the end I will sink
Into the nothing which is everything,   170
To find continuous resurrection
Of light into darkness, dark into light,
And know everything, which will show
That knowledge doesn't matter, isn't matter,
But all will be joined by a love passing knowledge.

* 1993

IT'S THE MOVEMENT DOES IT

I

Movement not stasis,
The movement counts and not the aim,
There our pleasure treasure lies:
Up and down, in and out.
If gold not change it is no better
Than the moth-corrupted cloth.
The sweet intense and momentary
Transition of desire to full
Completion, combination of,
Comparison, of states
Of feeling; hunger, being fed;
Release as of a bullet from the now,
Immediate hitting of the target
Of the then, two sorts
Of consciousness alive at once,
The moment in between when we
Are both united and apart,
Aware of both the after and before,
Essentially alive as transitory.
Getting and spending is the fertile way.
Having been cold, to be warm will do,
Even if hungry; it's better getting drier
Than wetter; growing up would be
Better than being mature, but
Maturity's ripeness rots
And may taste better.

l. 2. Edward Bernstein

II

It is tiring to decide.
Why not let the stream take us?
Rippling water as we float
Gives illusion of movement
Chosen not inevitable.
Can you change the banks,
Significantly alter speed,
Staunch the inevitable
All-conquering seepage?
Avoid the waterfall?
Make the sun shine?
Still it seems a pity
Only to be still.

DREAMS

That dwarf Consciousness, inside my head,
At dawn runs out along his dim jetty
At the edge of the dark tumultuous sea,
Against my will to haul half-broken nets
With their misshapen fish, threshing a moment,
Before their mad brightness dulls,
While the slowing surges that they wandered in
Tug at the jetty's struts, and the dwarf weeps,
And giggles, taking them home for his breakfast.

ON A PARK BENCH

What are they doing there, sitting still
While yellow leaves curl slowly down,
Together on a bench, holding hands
Warm palm to palm in the cold?
The wind is getting colder. He grey haired, and she
  not young,
In a thin dull coat. They kiss,
And a warm breeze ruffles the stagnant pond.

It is as it is

THE GATES OF GAZA

*In the Middle Ages the episode of Samson carrying off the gates of Gaza,
Judges 16, was taken as an antitype of Christ harrowing hell to release
those damned because born before the Redemption. Modern exegetes take it
as a folktale – Hebron was too far away to carry the gates.*

I

You've got to laugh when you think
Of bully-boy Samson full of insolence and lust
Plunging at night into his enemy whore in the middle
Of the town, too; and the men not men enough
To take him by darkness, in the darkness of his thrust.
'Let him wait; we catch him in dawn's ordinary light,
Unable then to stand to, weakened by the sport
And spurt of sex, locked in by sleep and gates'.
But he, giant refreshed by sweet labour, sprang out
At night, hulking the gates from hinges, shouldering   10
His way in derision and triumph
                                   – bizarre similitude
To turn upon one sharp point alone – what genius saw
What breakout meant; the lout as infernal harrower?
Identity dissolves: only the act
In isolation, free to mean, remains,
To all interpreters an open gate
Without restraint, the killing letter killed.

And so you dried-up exegetes chose spunky Samson.
Wild freedom draws those still immured.   20
Your minds and hearts lusted to roam.
You needed the trickster, the self-justifying self,
The mighty fornicator with foreigners, riddler, puzzler,
Who broke lion's jaws, nature's laws, rules and gates
(Hebron too far, our serious modernist says,
For anyone to carry those gates) – O solemn scholars,
No doubt bald and bespectacled, respectable and literal,
You need the madness of those ancient expositors
Who saw that words need not be true to be true,
That meat can come out of the eater, sweetness from
    strength   30
That virtue embraces its contrary in miraculous
    conception,
That parallel lines can meet for a moment
And righteous unlucky Gaza is itself a Hell.

II

From the beginning he was wanted by some, announced 40
In flames of fire, came in the usual river of blood, rolled
Down to become a stumbling block on the borders.
He was a hurricane who sated drought with excess,
A torrent of waters that roamed over the desert,
Who gathered the women in armfuls; they loved it.
He tore the lion apart, made it a hive and robbed it   40
Of honey disdaining petty stings. Silky sweet was
    his tongue,
His mind made knots to tangle the young men
And he won his bets, and tied fire to foxes' tails,

And the night covered him in a garment of lion skin
And he burst the bonds of the treacherous women
   he loved
And his hair was as the land's shade from the sun.
When they reaped it his might dried up like a river
   in summer.
Time, blindness, grief, refertilised,
And the trickster turned circus performer played
His last trick and brought down the house.   50

III

Welcome the wildness of these images, but trust
   them not.
Earthbound they crawl and sway like battle-tanks,
The drivers mad, half-blind, the spawn of history,
Who drive like drunks each vehicle,
To crush our learned ignorance, explode our
   preconceptions,
The tenor perched on top, precarious, vulnerable,
To sing strange messages
In languages we guess at, intimations barely heard,
Riding on that worldly vehicle (whose grinding word
May be itself part of the tenor's song) to crash at last   60
In some dry valley, killing the driver, while
The singer rises up above the ruined word
To sing a threnody of hope beyond all hope,
Free from the bonds of meaning's rotting flesh.

IV

Most gates are good
Some to shut out
Some to shut in
And those who build them
Have faith and mean
Them to last, boundaries   70
For the enemy without
And within. If no boundary,
Where are you? I need to know.
If no boundary, where am I?
What defence, what control?
We slither and overflow,
We lose ourselves.
Nowhere to return to,
When he tore off the gates
And carried them away   80
To mock us in law-abiding Gaza.
But the law makes sin,
And boundaries bind.
If we wish, we can be free.

V

To see resemblance in wild difference,
To note how in the river of mud and destruction
There lives the seed of the Son-flower;
That vice as manliness (too true)
May image divine revocation
Of an ancient divine justice which   90

24

Unjustly made just to be born a sin;
That took a weird exegetical genius
A Kierkegaard come to judgment, before his time.

VI

Dare we follow, find, the true new now,
Follow new Samson come to higher judgment?
Story him, not store; break old meanings,
Open new: suppose all but safety? Gates
Have no guarantee but to lock us in
Not him. We ourselves our own hell.
Leave him liberator, life's laughter at logic,   100
Destroyer of old, and of self.

ll. 52–6. Apart from allusions to the text of Judges 16 the expressions 'tenor' and 'vehicle' originate in the analysis of metaphor: the 'vehicle' is the literal sense, the 'tenor' its metaphorical implications.

1999

SUCH STUFF

I dreamt I walked on Birmingham station
Under a dome of dirty-coloured glass;
A stranger came to me of unknown nation,
And in the din made no attempt to pass.

He walked familiarly with me of all the crowd:
'I'm Death', he said, and as I went to speak
He added in a friendly way, not loud,
'I'll meet you here for good within the week'.

And then with longer pace he hurried on,
But looked a little round; 'So long, old chap!'
'*Old* chap!' I cried, before he had quite gone,
'There's some mistake. I've not yet lost my sap'.

And so he checked before going on his way.
A figure spry and middle-aged and slight,
And turned to me a face of human gray –
My face I saw beneath that smoke-stained light.

But this was all a month ago or more,
And mornings as I scrape that face of mine
I say to him, 'You *are* a bloody bore';
I laugh at him and say, 'Be off, you swine'.

Doubt not; go forward

THE TREE OF LIFE

Adam and Eve sweated and worked, groaned, laughed,
On the whole prospered, and had some good some bad
Times, children, family quarrels, disasters and reunions;
Achieved their house; bought a car, went out
For a drink at weekends; visited grandchildren,
Grew fat, complained of the immorality of the young:
Their shame familiar, compatible and warm
As the old, good clothes that followed the fig-leaves,
Though covering a medicated sore.
Knowledge itself was good, if even of evil.   10
Knowledge to dig and grow, to store, increase
And multiply (especially by computer) and then
Advance technology. Then understand?
Then Adam had a heart attack.

Within the pulsing mass
That gives the quick of life
The insistent clot can't pass,
Blood with itself at strife.

The doctor (himself a great-great-grandson) explained the mechanism of
the body and the hopes of spare-part surgery. Eve was anxious and
indignant. How could the heart that loved her be exchanged; Adam
divided from himself? 'The knowledge that you bought', advised the doctor
cheerfully (he was still young), 'fortunately allows us to postpone death – at
least, while the younger population allows' (he added warningly).

'I see', said Adam, recognising both
The good and bad; but all the same was loth   20
To think that all his life was come to this,
A worn-out engine driving to the abyss.
There was a time when there had seemed more choice
Among the chances, and a warmer voice.

*The doctor said, 'You need some change, and much more exercise; travel, to
distract the mind'. 'What I need', said Adam, 'is less change, or not to
have changed. But I will travel to discover my mind.'*

The infinite electrical complexities
Within the skull then struck a bell,
But that reverberation lost its path;
Yet images that seemed to hesitate
Like fishes quivering in clear water
That with a flick are lost, yet come again   30
From under the dark rocks and vaguely
Floating coloured weed, above the sifted sand,
Awoke in Adam's mind a seeking hope,
Not knowing what it looked to, that he might
Recover yet a loss of which he'd lost
The very sense of loss. He would go back.

*So, briskly, fat and faithful Eve, with a good wife's sceptical indulgence of
husbands' fanciful schemes, packed up.*

The car was loaded, guidebooks, biscuits, a bottle
Or two (only one of doctor's medicine),
For emergencies sleeping bags, and a torch,
Water-can, matches, some crockery and tins of meat,   40

For that sweet wilderness which they were looking for
Had no hotels when they were young.

But as it proved the problems were not such.
The car ran well and petrol-pumps
Like trees in multi-coloured groves festooned
The motorways that sliced the desert
And the town, the tundra, mountain, meadows, woods,
All passing like a film, seen from persistent
Though quivering seats: no smells or sounds except
Their own until the engine stopped upon   50
A side road where they were quite lost. The silence spoke,
A healing nothingness: Eve said, 'We must
Get on'. Soon they were back to catch a plane,
Encapsulated in its noise, strapped down
Above the world, its scents and sounds and feelings.

Adam and Eve looked from the empyrean
Down to the chain-gang of the human race,
Irrevocably linked in generation,
In needs of love and hate. Men carried gifts
Of various use and value, valued variously,   60
As spades or jewels, compasses, big sticks,
With which they helped and beat, cajoled and tempted
Others. Some stared lost, no gift to carry,
Fallen and trodden on, or pulled by friends.
Others were burdened with such wealth
That they were crippled, while the rest snatched up
For fame and fortune the forgotten jewels
That had dripped through their fingers.
And some were hugging to themselves what soon

Would crush them and roll off, to be picked up,   70
Or kicked, by others. Most were anxious, few
Serene. 'What has gone wrong?' said Adam. 'Did
We begin like this?' He turned inward to look.

Adam remembered waking from his dream
Of desire, to see beside him on soft grass the girl
With golden hair, naked in the glorying sun.
They walked in splendour down the wooded valley
In the first spring of all, bright trees, new grass,
A stream where tigers calmly drank, and birds
To watch them stayed and sang, and violets   80
Were glowing signals by the pool and falling
Waters. To be was then to love as one,
In unity the meeting of desire.

'And that was knowing', Adam said aloud.
Said Eve, 'Ignorance rather, until we did
Some Research, and found how little known,
In conscious self-awareness to possess,
Could joy be until lost. You cannot classify
When you're inside the class. Significance,
The wisest thinkers say, essentially   90
Is adventitious value, not inherent.
The independent human mind itself
Creates its values. Joy can only be
Known in sadness, good by bad. Remember
As salutary pain, chosen necessity,
The dropping into cold, the rainy stroke
Of lightning breaking through the darkened veil
Of innocence.'

'Who could forget' said Adam,
'Yet in remembrance not obliterate   100
That primal worst expulsion, the nakedness
Upon the cold unstirring earth? To find
The everlasting fruits, bright scenes that filled
The mind with ever-fresh familiar joy,
Exchanged for rocks, the seasons' painful wheel;
To wander seeking home like exiles through
A world empty of all but us and those like us,
No visitants of spirit who could validate
Intuitive reliance on the sense
And goodness made by being in itself.'   110

Said Eve, 'A Paradise can only be
Inhabited by fools who do not know
Its bliss. We lost it with our ignorance
But now we know it through our loss, though how
And to what human purposes we must
Find out.'
                    Said Adam, 'That's our ignorance still.'
'We have discovered Time', said Eve, 'and that
Will bring all things.'
                              'Including', Adam added,   120
'Death, that takes all things away from us.'

A choice was made now long ago
Between two fruits;
We re-enact the lust to know,
Examining our roots.

The satisfaction of that choice,
Who can deny?
It drugged us to forget the voice
That said, we die.

It was not ordinary greed   130
That led us then:
The act was in our given seed,
That made us men.

Our fault was not in our excess,
Once we exceeded,
But that we were content with less
That what we needed.

The choice we made to do and know
Was incomplete
If so to multiply and grow   140
Is but defeat.

No inward prohibition stopped,
No flaming knife;
It was our own obsession cropped
Knowledge, not life.

The plane now circled round the blessed spot
Of former home, and greybeard Adam hid
His face.
              'O good!' said Eve. 'I see the Hilton.
The earth that was so naked is now clothed   150
In concrete: housing, offices and shops

Are guaranteed by cooling-towers, array
Of chimneys, and a cider-factory.
Bright lights and noise declare prosperity.
The desert and the silence, darkness of the night,
Are conquered like the reluctant earth.
Women here are free from pain of childbirth,
And free too from the dread of bearing children
Into this suffering world.'

       'Where is the Tree?' 160
Said Adam.

     'Over there' said Eve, 'a forest
Grown from our fruitful plucking flourishes
Well-planned and regular, spaced out, controlled,
And properly guarded.'

      'But where', said Adam,
'Is the other, that we did not pluck and should have,
Not being forbidden but by wantonness?'

There seemed no sign, but as he asked
The plane dropped, the concrete heaved, the

        suffering earth 170
Roared and cracked, and from the cracks a voice
That cried, to break the maternal heart of Eve:
 'You have chosen to know
 You know good by evil;
 You know joy by suffering;
 You know being by doing'
 You know life by death.
 You cannot go back;
 Do not give up;
 Go on.'   180

Adam pulled Eve from the wreckage; both were dying.
And Adam cried out, as amongst the fires
That raged around he saw the Tree of Life.
Splintered, with only a couple of boughs,
But bearing as fruit a man like others,
But a fruit to be eaten, nevertheless. And Adam
Was dying and could not reach, could not go back.
This time the fruit, that was his, and Eve's, and them.
Could not be taken, unless it should
Choose itself, should descend and come to them.   190

They gave thanks and died.

                                                      * 1972

PRISONERS OF OUR TIME

A little to the left or right, up and down –
Not quite tied down: an inclination of
The head; derisive gesture of big toe.
Who says we have no freedom? We can sing,
When something unconstrainable wells up
Within us prisoners, escaping knotted sinews
Clotted bowels, caging ribs. But generally
We're tied, roped round and round by history,
Past decisions, manacled by constraints
We didn't choose, and others that we did,
Those locks and bars we call ourselves. We lie,
In every sense, quite quietly, most of the time,
Or try to move a little closer in the darkness,
And whisper strange words, make signals no one
   understands.
The constant general murmur has its groans,
But now and then, some idiot sings, and breaks
Into a light and freedom that we only guess,
And makes us think we might know other lives.

CONSTRAINT – ANOTHER VIEW

The river is no river if its flow
Be not constricted, banked, intensified,
The channel deepened though it roar with pain.
To not get all you want is what you are.

THE REVERSE OF AN AUBADE

Just risen from her bed, upon the stair
She stood above him, smiling at the air.
He from outside, below, half conscious of defeat,
'Will you come walking? – see how this June's heat
Brings out the roses' – She touches tousled hair;
Another one to pick the rose was there.

OBLIVION

Oblivion must be best.
Since ignorance is such pain,
Not to know one does not know,
Doubly deprived, we gain.

No one had told me this was what to expect

MAGNA MATER

ORIGINS

Motherhood, primeval mystery:
Mounded ashes, fire without smoke,
Star of the sea, lily of the valley,
A moon to wax and wane for ever,
Pregnant like white veined quartz, or filled sea-shells.
Carved alabaster filled with light.
Glass pierced with a ray of heaven,
Winged Madonna, laying the silver egg
Which holds all things: beehive
Full of sweetness, labour and stings;   10
Triadic virgin mother and crone;
O bulging pot, shattered by discontented contents,
Resistant to our hold, ever inviting embrace,
Evading male rank and order,
Carving and coiling away and round them,
Controlling by fleeing, dominating by succumbing,
How shall men need you and speed you,
Believe you and leave you,
Find home where you are not,
Avoid the castrating love, reverse your growth   20
In order to grow in freedom,
Solving the mystery by a new death?[2]

2 Robert Graves, *The Greek Myths*, Harmendsworth, 1960, Introduction,
   ch.1 6.

CYBELE

Great mother of gods
Engendering and devouring.
Ask Attis where he comes from.
What is now his pallid life,
Burnt-out son-Father?
What sacrifice you take.
Where and what are your daughters –
Do you hide them from us?   30
You draw us in to cut off what only you can give,
Sucking up where you have given suck;
Great spider of love,
Tormenting us with need.
We drown in the blood of bulls,
In our own sperm, all light
Of mind lost in the fecund ditch.[3]

PIERO'S MADONNA DELLA MISERICORDIA

The cloak will draw us in
To sweet-smelling female warmth,
Out of the cold world's wind,   40
To give us mercy, if only we
Will stay on our knees in the dark.
We worship you, mother, together;
Why should we turn away?

---

3 Graves and *Oxford Classical Dictionary*, s.v. Attis, Cybele.

Piero's Madonna del Parto

Pregnant goddess at the gate of death
Bursting with futurity at the end of time,
Mother-to-be of the dissolving corpse,
Turning death into life and life into death:
What comfort is offered to men
As we slide back to the womb of the tomb.[4]   50

Give us space

Magnet and martyr
Suffering and acting,
Drawing repelling,
Mindless old woman, unmindful young,
Pregnant with promise, cloaking the old,
Womb and tomb of all we know,
Your ejection of us is our rejection
Necessary painful salvation,
Birth that is death, to give us
A moment of our own in between   60
To make another mother.

Where shall we go from here?

Once opened door forever left behind,
To which the backward look is death: Pluto's realm
Of darkness, warmth; volcanic origin

4 The great painting of the pregnant Virgin was originally in a small
chapel by a cemetery. Now alas it is in a little museum of art history by
the side of the road from Arezzo to Borgo San Lorenzo, all *numen* gone.

That flung us into open air, to sun and star.
We are smoke and dust, lava flow; destruction
Is our own creation till we cool
And stiffen in another kind of death.
What are we, so useless, undirected,
Taking the easiest direction of flow,   70
In burning ourselves burning others,
Tormented in coiling passion, to escape
From which is only to escape ourselves
In no transcendence but mere mindlessness?

REPROACHES [5]

O Mummy, Mummy, what have you done to me?
See my wounds bleed. Where have you led me to?
What burden was I to you, that this burden you place
   on me?
Your suffering from me loads me with more.
No suckling, no succour can come here for me.
That absent father never will rescue me.   80
No angels can bear me.
Leave me mother, where you have brought me,
Cast off all care for me,
Here alone must I be, only me.

PROGRESS

Bare bony truth is, we must die. The flesh
Of metaphor corrupts 'beyond the grave'.

---

5 The Reproaches are a parallel of those from the Cross spoken on
   Good Friday.

No dry bone lives; eat flesh, drink blood,
Let fancy rise with flesh and blood.
No truth in them that perish, no support.
To live needs guts.   90
Let us eat and drink, then, flesh and blood,
Accept, reject, eject,
And love well if not wisely just to live,
To be the things we are. 'Dry light is best'
Said Bacon: – Give me darkness, warm and wet,
The mother's breast, the woman's thighs,
And to be merry: truth will not stay to answer . . .

Nor will the rest. Mothers will die, and lovers
Deny, deceive, depart. Images decay like flesh.

But why should we despair? To be denied   100
At least is to have asked: hunger and thirst
Show our capacities for life. Departure depends
On previous presence, fullness needs desire,
Desire creates the fantasising lust,
The sense of loss we do not wish to lose.

PIERO'S RESURRECTION

Out of the wintry diagonal landscape,[6]
Foot on the hard tomb's straight line,
With soldiers asleep or amazed,
In sloppy curves, at first light,
When it is time to stand to,[7]   110

6 The picture is Piero's Resurrection in Borgo San Lorenzo.
7 'Stand to' is the period just before and after dawn when attack is most likely
   and soldiers in a fortified position must awake to take up defensive positions.

All worldly comfort gone or spurned,
With clear mathematical gaze,[8]
Unmoved you take the real world's measure,
And fly your banner coolly.
Where is mother now?

ABSORPTION

No future here: to live is now; but not
To look for comfort from the others. We
Are the sons, the daughters too, who eat
The father: the mother gives us suck,
But now we drink to suck her up. It's we   120
Who give the breast and clothe and carry loads
And take the sword that penetrates the heart.
The mother is no longer great: but us.

IN CONCLUSION

Through myths we live,
We live through myths
To achieve the ordinary wonder
By wondering at the ordinary.
Death is no solution,
Only dissolution,
Stand fast and fly your flag.   130

1982

8 Piero della Francesca is notable for the underlying mathematical
   structure of his paintings.

FATHERS

Many men (and no doubt I)
Are like a sleepy pear:
The skin's all right; no fly
Upon it, but the core
Is mushy; we've no reasons why
We'd stand the stake, the fire,
As men did once – some now – at need:
We only justify ourselves by seed.

Always different: always the same

ETERNAL FEMININE

I

As beautiful and young as you may be
You also are the ancient woman-house,
Ramshackle, always added to, that stands
The same for centuries, shelters our dreams, desires.
You welcome strangers who will come to stay
But do not keep their promise. Others come
Who go unwillingly. Some knock and are
Not answered, while you lose your way and feel
Afraid. Others sweep through and keep
You from yourself, your inner room and joy.
And there are other rooms where children sleep,
And one, to whose locked door you keep the key,
Whose drab bare walls are splashed with blood.
Yet company strange and varied fills the house
In motley colours. It is founded on
No sand or rock bur floats in water, life
And death. The gondolas swim through with song.
The people work or laze, all gaze at you,
Who in yourself, distracted yet at home,
Hospitable to others yet in search
Of self and of that Other who is none
Of us: your one opposing dreaded self,
Who comes inexorably for reckoning.
Demands the key to see the room.

II

But was it wise to seek that inner room?
Will not the Bearded One return and you
Be caught with blood upon your hands of all
Your earlier selves he butchered; virgin, wife,
Who suffered loss, betrayal, murder; which
You had no choice but leave within locked up?
Would you relive the past? Must not the self
Leave loss behind, the dead to bury the dead,
Be active, seeking, restless, anxious, as
You are? Identity is fixed, but life
Is movement, seeking, in the present, tense.

(The reference is to the story of Bluebeard.)

IN MEMORIAM R.G. 1920–97

I do not mourn for my old friend whom death
Has now relieved of senseless life. I mourn
For his lost youth and old friends still alive
Whom now I meet, not seen for forty years,
The stiff baldheaded men who once jumped stiles,
Proud-bosomed grandmothers, *Grandes Dames*,
Who once were thin girls laughing on their bikes.
They flirted long with Time, who married them,
They call him and each other 'Dear'. But Time
Has scratched his marks upon our faces, thinned
Our legs and swelled our paunch and scraped our hair
And dried our skin, in preparation for
The fire in which we throw mortality,
Nirvana of annihilation for
Us all. We old can easily be spared.
It is our youth we mourn, the rising sap,
Green hills, the music and the kisses and the wine,
The perishable objects of our love,
And only youth is what we really loved.
But we must leave behind youth, love and life,
And goodness, innocence and sacrifice.
Give thanks for all; death is our last best friend.

PETER WYLD, 1920–99

And Peter Wyld is dead whom bullets, bombs
And enemy could not kill, though he killed them,
Now more than fifty years ago. The least aggressive man,
Who showed how names may still traduce the truth,
He never spoke of war to us who had survived,
But was the most polite, the gentlest, humorous
Of clever men without ambition or
A thought of self, as shown in that fierce fight,
In which he led attacks with such cruel zest
That burnt from him the need to overcome,
Though brilliant the need to shine, excel,
Except in being just himself, just man in deed.
But what then should he do? He laughed and with
One leg he walked the world, danced with the Queen
With all the grace that came to him and took
His orders from a higher source, remained
His own man at the service of us all.

*Peter Wyld was at the beginning of World War II a conscientious objector
who eventually joined the Army. He won a Military Cross for bravery,
was blown up by a mine and lost a foot. On his return after the war as an
undergraduate to Magdalen College, Oxford, he took a brilliant First in
English, wandered the world doing odd jobs for a year or two, then took
Holy Orders.*

I form the light and create darkness;
I make peace and create evil:
I am the Lord that doeth
all these things.

DEUS ABSCONDITUS
VARIATIONS ON A THEME

I

AWAKENING

On the surrounding hills no detail could be seen,
all was a smooth deep dull blue. Above the hills was a
paler equally undifferentiated sky. Then at the skyline
an intense fiery spark sprang out. The spark turned
into a fierce eye, sending its ray to see what we were
up to, whether we were awake. Then the eye turned
into an immense glowing orange ball, more benign,
blander, seeing that perhaps we were not up to very
much, or caring less about it. The earth meanwhile
was turning itself more and more towards the great
ball, yearning towards it, opening itself up to its
influence, adoring it. The ball rose, becoming more
intense, further away, concerned with higher things.
Brightness and shadows came to the earth. The sun
was more remote, in the hard blueness, you could
look at it no longer, it burnt impersonally. Clouds
came. Daylight was all around; it seemed to come
from nowhere, it was merely the element in which we

lived and worked. Would we not have been happy to
continue so? But the night came.

II

LONG BARROW

Swells up on the hill's forehead a huge bruise;
This day's bland warmth cossets the lasting pain.
Poultices of earth and stone seal and save
Irrecoverable loss. Tourists now peer
Inside the sacral burial chamber, where once lay
Fifteen adults and six children; men, women, servants.
Now dogs and children ramble over. Parents
Protest and puff, throw down their plastic waste,
Dislodge the dry-stone walls, and pick the flowers;
A sunny motoring Sunday's picnic treat.   10
Three thousand years ago a sombre crowd
Equally contemporary, far less clean,
Then brought the king's body, brightly wrapped,
With labour up the slope, proclaimed their loss
And fear, drove up his servants, pages, women,
Slaughtered them to give him fitting services,
(Raping the women first, not to be wasteful)
Piled high the earth, shrieked higher to their gods;
The illustrious corpse thus honoured and propitiated,
They turned to muddy huts in hope to have   20
At least saved harvest, kept their families.
They'd spent an interesting afternoon,
And kept in touch with deity,
Like us, as we drive home past cemeteries.

III

A Modernist Psalm

Before everything that is,
    Thou wast:
Unto thee all things proceed.
    Thou has created all things
    and all things rest in thee,
At the centre of the universe, thou   30
    art there,
And at the rim of infinite space
    there art thou also.
When I look into my heart
    I find thee.
Upon thee all my values depend,
My passions arise out of thee, and my
convictions are based on the knowledge
    of thee,
I walk in thy ways, and my   40
    friends join me in contemplating thee:
My terror is great when I think upon
    thee, and yet fear need be none:
It is easy to forget you, Ground
    of our Being,
Being Nothing.

IV

The landscape is packaged: heavy wires hold
Us together, humming with transferred energies

As they hold us down with urgent messages,
As they hold us up with hope of gain   50
And power, of richer, brighter, louder lives.
The wasteful hedgerows and meandering paths,
Useless crinkles making untidy parcels
Will be smoothed out. Meanwhile like rotten teeth
Within an old man's mouth,
Decaying, yellow, jagged, stand out church towers
Above the gaping windows in unkempt graveyards,
Recalling aching joys for other mouths.

V

THE CATHEDRAL

It is the mind, the mind, that makes these stones
Holy, that turns them into bread for minds   60
That chew through sedimentary
Depths, sinking through ancient swarming seas
To swirling mass and gas, through molecule
Atom, proton, neutron and the first
Intimate throb, embodied energy,
Minute infinitude, bounded in clay,
Electrical discharge. The exploring mind
Now turns on its own nature, destroys
The bread it fed on, breaks the stones, requires
A brutal hammer, holystones the kitchen   70
Floor with sacred images, rubs the nose
Of loving art in gross necessity
Of cleansing dirt of common intercourse.
Now cleanliness will be our godliness.

The mind will seek a purer empyrean
In the smooth plane and calm of abstract thought.

VI

O throw away those hours
Of youth like faded flowers
Accept the new condition
Of contempt and suspicion.   90

The landscape shrinks within a frame,
The river of blood is tame,
A tree may flower in stars but down
Beneath, a lonely clown.

A cold light shows the dust upon the bleak
Interior and on your cheek.
A pistol-shot – a scream –
The dim portrait smiles within its dream;

Its glass is broken
And as a doubtful token   100
A half-heard tune is cast
Between the future and the past.

O throw away those hours
Of youth like faded flowers
Now newly comes the season
Of regrets and reason.

VII

Within my mind a strangeness penetrates
The edges of perception – as in a room
At night the dawn makes slowly grayly visible
The outlines of a furniture unknown,   110
A window to an empty sea, a shiny sand,
A faint blue sky with one last star, a wind,
A scent from unknown woods and fields,
An expectation and a hush in which
One solitary unknown bird tries out
Preliminary notes before – who comes?

VIII

THE SPRING

That scent comes like a message, fresh, half-heard,
Each spring, never to be traced, like a bird
Whose song always is just to pass;
The balsam-poplar, may, or growing grass,   120
Uncertain and poignant, evasive, leaves
That whisper a scent, asking, who grieves?

IX

Pine smoke poignant scent
Through cool night-air blown,
Fire-given long youth ago,
Recollected now, same stars
Still watching as it fades.

X

DECEMBER THRUSH

What can he mean by it? Trilling
So early, hopefully, as if it were spring,
Yet the leaves are almost lost, the last   130
Rose utterly sogged. True, mornings are mild,
Not like the last, this winter. Still no frost,
No paradoxical midwinter spring. Yet
The thrush sings a practised note, not
Young and ignorant, but ripe, throbbing,
It wakes us, unaccustomed on these dark mornings
To hopeful variations on a theme
We had thought gone with summer.

XI

Galapagos! Galapagos!
There the biologist seeks his dream.   140
Of two million forms of insect life
There alone are six which live at sea;
Unknown their habits, the cycle of their lives
Unregistered in books since Darwin first
Made notes. A project worth the Royal's grant
To study them and fit them into evolution's scale,
To bring them into Nature's scheme.
But what he looks for is an emptiness.
The work is worthy, will get done; and yet
The waking on the deck at dawn, the sun   150
To rise over the calmly heaving sea,

Beside the remote volcano's silent crest
And whisp of smoke; the filling sail; steersman,
No English spoken, standing darkly by,
The water gurgling at the larboard strake;
That inexpressible communication
Is what he goes to listen for.

XII

Another, grave and reverend senior,
Inhabiting a high dry room of books and wooden chairs,
Cannot keep his hands off girls   160
Who come to learn – what mysteries?
What does *he* seek? – two questions there.
One answer is like all we know,
Less interesting than the ignorance
Of that deeper mystery that evades his hands.

XIII

O lonely old couple, keeping warm around
The fading fire, the children long departed,
The clouds hurrying to darken the moon,
To bring the rain to slash against the windows,
What will you do now the dark-coated stranger   170
Knocks at the door? Is there a chance of keeping
Him out? Does charity tell you to open
The door, to let in all the cold blasts
Of the world? And as he knocks again, again,
Will the door stand his battering? Or will
He set fire to the walls, bringer of hell?

Will he faint from hunger and cold if you
Wait long enough, if you can? You look
At each other. The wind blows indoors, light fades,
Each of you a dark-coated stranger, inside the house. 180

XIV

The details of the plain slowly faded; greens and
brown turned to grey, houses, barns, roads became
unfocussed, a mist spread evenly over the lower
ground. The bare hills caught a warmer light than
they deserved and the clouds were fired to a sullen
red till they eventually turned a bluish-grey, and they
too lost their identity, as all merged in silence. A
small star appeared. Others came scattered like silver
seed: rather, like chinks of light in the high
empyrean that covers us over. We know they are not
that. Terror seizes us to contemplate the silence of
those eternal frozen spaces. Is fear the beginning of
wisdom? We cannot hear the voices which first spoke
such words. But silent echoes in the greater space of
mind, as night falls, sleep comes, teach us some
divine discomfort.

* 1980

YOUTH

... Like some sailor on his shipwrecked raft
Who suddenly is caught up in
The surging wave and flung
Upon a warm and gentle shore,
Left gasping half-dissolved in bed.

YOUNG LOVE

Last night I had a winsome dream,
My girl lay in my arm.
Then she gave out a fearful scream
– It was my clock's alarm.

Ah what harsh wakening was there,
To dawn and lonely bed,
To tedious daytime wear and care.
The girl that never was had fled.

But then I thought my choice was made
Of freedom light and space,
Of bacon, eggs and marmalade.
I sought no further grace.

GLASTONBURY

This vale is fertilised with blood and tears,
A marsh where men and women like us though
Much less well-off, shorter lived, worshipful,
Had houses over the lake, and when massacred
Left their blood to enrich, and perhaps stories,
Of Avalon and healing apples from
Where now are pasture and orchards and ruins.
Alfred, England's darling, wandered in marshes here,
Pursued, disconsolate, and dropped his jewel
But fought and found another jewel, England.
The great Dunstan, founder, reviver of churches,
A foundryman at his forge in his cell.
He tore the Devil's nose off when at his forge,
With his tongs. He hammered his own soul
Into red-hot iron at the furnace of his own mind.
The last of the abbots, Richard Whiting,
Let him always be honoured, would have done
The same to the King, royal looter and ruiner,
If he could, but the king was no devil,
But a man who was stronger and Cromwell said
We will try Richard Whiting and guilty we'll find him.
And Richard stood on the hill over meadows,
That high hill holy to many,
And for doing his duty was called a robber,
A robber of what was entrusted to him,
For keeping it from the robber-King,
For which he was hanged and his body quartered,
As traitor to the King though not to God,
And his head, testifying faith, was staked

As a guardian over the gate, to warn others not
To be so stiff-necked; while fabulous Arthur,
Deep-tombed below, a king for his people,
Groaned in his false grave confirmed by the true King.
But Richard stood true to a higher King.
Do not forget him and all those like him,
As you walk in the ruins and climb the hill,
Unpersecuted, comfortable among
The so-called souvenirs and tourist junk
Which suffering has now made possible.

On the history referred to see James P. Carley, Glastonbury Abbey, *The Boydell Press, Woodbridge, 1988.*

I have left aside the fables of Joseph of Arimathea bringing Christianity and the Holy Grail in 63, but Glastonbury in Somerset was thought of as Avalon, island of apples, and early people lived there in lake-dwellings. Alfred at the lowest ebb of his fortunes took refuge in the marshes of Somerset and the famous gold-enamelled jewel with the words in Old English 'Alfred caused me to be made' was found there near Athelney, perhaps dropped by him, 877–8. St Dunstan (c. 909–88) was a celebrated worker in gold, hence the legend of his seizing the Devil by the nose with a pair of red-hot tongs. He became Abbot of Glastonbury in 945 and became Archbishop of Canterbury, 959, and led the revival of the Benedictine Rule for monks.

What were claimed to be the bodies of King Arthur and Queen Guinivere were solemnly interred before the High Altar in the presence of Edward I in 1278, implying that Edward was Arthur's legitimate successor. The splendid tomb was destroyed at the Reformation, along with so much else.

Unselfishness and loyalty
are not natural.

Iris Murdoch

ANIMA NATURALITER CHRISTIANA

PART ONE

Cranmer

I carry Cranmer as a burden in
My mind, with Ridley, Latimer and all
Women and men, serious, convinced, convicted,
Who die with shuddering flesh against the grain,
Making 'I would not' go against the wood,
Which burns the body to release the soul.

*

They tore off the archbishop's robes to dress
Him in clownish rags; badgered him, burrowed
Into his reasons. He courteously stuck,
Defended, pedantically considered,   10
An old man prisoned, whom the Queen determined
Must in justice die for his absurd belief
That she was God's executant. Her pride
Was her humility, her power refusal
Of such power. Seven times his recantation
Exceeded recantation, forced back continually,
By inch and inch gave ground until his inner
Lair seemed open. He was dug out and up.
Surrender meant death not release; all lost
To God, whose power he would have granted to 20

The Queen, who so refused it as to order death
For his agreement with her theologian hounds.
To God the honour and the glory; God
Himself decreed his death, his failure as a scholar;
Decreed destruction for the Church he'd built;
His friends betrayed, humiliation with
One end if in the end God's will prevail.
But what that end may be is still unknown.

*

But when all's lost he's free. He gives
A mighty precedent, not without precedent.   30
'Let this cup pass from me', but not if your will
Is to thrust it down my throat, an old bewildered man,
Who suddenly sees the bonfire light,
Which no cup quenches but which feeds the flame.
New light refires conviction's strength.
New freedom comes to lighten Englishmen.
The Queen, God's chosen hand as he believed,
Until she forced on him old unbelief,
Herself made Cranmer great in death, to show
How Christians unnaturally may die,   40
Transcend their substance in a natural way.

The coming drink of death quenched natural thirst.
The bitter taste of Mary clarified
The murky spurious nostrums he'd outgrown.
No drug to drown the pain but purity
Of clear intent and purpose must be drunk.
She wished to burn his soul, not body alone,
And England's new soul. He was refreshed,
Released from doubt; no saint, though a good man;

Reluctant martyr; for he found himself   50
Unnaturally made better than himself.

To the stake they led him, prepared, they thought,
To speak his utter self-abasement. Two
Scripts he had, 'of comfort and despair',
Divided mind, the scholar's *pro* and *con*.
Then mind and sky cleared bright and glorious.
Recanted recantation stood to it like a man,
For Ridley, Latimer, the scholar-friends,
Who at the Eagle once held earnest talk,
And, called to act, imposed their thought and will   60
On others (who equally had suffered death,
For spirit mattered more than matter then.)

They'd willed a new Church on the multitude
Of average sensual men (by nature
Not zealous, mostly willing to worship
God through King or Queen or noble images
– As near God as good nature cared to come –)
They'd willed to make men think against the grain,
To hurt their minds, to break the customary bond,
The comfortable inclusive natural law.   70
Now such men crowded round in natural lust,
To hear the expected grovelling words, to see
Old Cranmer burn, at last his true conclusion.

The Queen had made the old man watch his friends,
Those fiery preachers, Ridley and Latimer,
See how their words were matched with other fire,
Their bodies like great candles spurting fat,

A light for England for long years to come,
Encouragement to others in a way
She had not realised when Cranmer watched   80
As Ridley's legs burnt off and boiling brains
Of learned scrupulous hotheads burst out their skull.
The crowd of natural women and men
Followed the curling arguments of smoke
And heard the crackle of the ancient flame,
They saw and heard no word of newer light.

Now Cranmer came to it and silence fell.
And he defied the Queen, accepted death,
To say 'I erred like a lost sheep, and here
My hand upon it, first to burn as err'.   90
That scholar's hand now wrinkles in the flame,
Smells not of midnight oil but roasted meat.

Then cheer on cheer the fickle multitude
Gave forth as slowly word by word they heard
And clearly understood his great revoke.

And now seemed gone, old logic's turns and twists,
And those old bodies too: yet clearly as
The screams, despite all will to silence, rose
Above the crackling wood, the message came
That friends were not betrayed, the wavering mind   100
Had made its great assertion that this day
A light again was lit that shone through clouds
Until the English thought Heaven not worth
     looking for.

*

Yet who would doubt that Mary acted in
Good faith, with Bonner, Pole, and all the rest?
This leaves the burning question still to ask.
Is burning such a natural Christian deed?
(Remembering Ridley preached before a pyre
Of one who did not share his own belief?)
To burn, in lust, in fever, or the foe   110
Seems natural indeed. Is Nature all?
If so, then Christianity is not.

PART TWO

Nature, you golden-hearted random slut,
Indifferent mother of pain, not cruel,
Because no moral consciousness is yours.
Promiscuously you generate our swarm.
Our birthstrings tangle us as we writhe
To escape – but with what impulse, for it's not
Your own? – our pullulating vital power.
No reason can be given. O where is He,   120
The Father strong and rational who knows
The laws of righteousness, to teach the way?
The Father and the Mother are divorced
Not only from each other but from us,
Who now can only fantasise their being,
We are alone, or so it seems, within
A transient bubble, varying in hue
Until it breaks to leave a mindless spot.

*

It cannot be said; it contradicts itself.
It's not enough to boast 'I contradict myself'.   130

64

And so some seek to find out where we are,
Asking 'Why?' and more insistently,
'Why not?' So from amoeba up to hominids
To men we puzzled on our way, except
That only few were puzzled. Most of us
Just struggled on for no more than to live
And mindlessly, though pleasurably,
(We wouldn't otherwise have tried so hard)
We reproduced our kind, not being kind.
Our nature (random unselfconscious choice)   140
Was but to dominate or to be cowed,
The strong in body and mind to be supreme,
To get the best and most out of our life.
The puzzled ones were still not satisfied,
The questioner was always there and asked
Such odd and different questions,
As, who, or what, was good, and 'Why?'; 'Why not?'.
And there our problem, because some more strong
Had answers which they forced on us. And some
Resisted; though why, when they could have   150
More comfortable life was not so clear.
Perhaps they only could be comfortable,
By self-assertion, even to their death.
A natural explanation. Self governs all
Even when it leads to total loss of self.
A fundamental egoism drives.
But some denied, and said we could not pull
Ourselves up by our own bootstraps; we need
Some transcendental holds outside ourselves.
Against that some said that we live gnats' lives   160
As in a rubber box, shared with the stars,

Down to the microbes, all produced by chance,
And there is no outside. That's all that is.
'There's nothing good or bad but thinking
Makes it so'. But that's absurd. Pain tells us so.
We 'find no end, in endless mazes lost'.
The questioner's the prisoner in the box.
All we can do is to deny the box,
The evidence of our senses to make sense,
Assert a grand hypothesis of love,   170
Of justice, mercy, that ourselves create.
Leave nature; deny her mastery,
For values are unknown in nature's box.

*

Let us praise goodness wherever we find it, though
Nature knows nothing of goodness. Let definitions
    swirl
Like swifts at dusk. Goodness may be what good men
    and women,
Or, as may be believed, all men and women,
(Do we need to say children too?) want most,
Is simply what they want, even if they hunger and
    thirst after
Righteousness, which seems unlikely and unnatural.   180
Let egoists at whatever skill, or whatever genius,
Perfect their lives or work, or try to, as they feel
Inclined. But for myself, I bear witness
That I have seen and known, (though not in myself),
But in mothers and friends, soldiers and those whose
    own loyalty
Sacrifice that was not subtle self-indulgence,
Which was hard, though its own reward,

Was chosen with pain and knowledge of lost joys
But freely chosen, recognising an outer goodness,
Which did not come from nature but knew itself,   190
Though the immediate effects might have seemed
    bad or good.
To try to be good is against the grain, and the chisel
    may slip,
But the work must be tried, the artefact made,
And though against nature may even improve or
    redeem it,
As souls may do, if there are souls,
Which are, we may say, by nature unnaturally
    Christian,
Or even just splendidly human.

*

If Mary had relented with success
With Cranmer having forced his shaking hand
To sign his recantations, then been freed,   200
As justice asked, would then the Queen have not
Attained her end and former practices
Of faith not kept their hold? What would we think
Of Cranmer then? A coward soul if not
Less Christian, and all too natural?
But when he saw that death could not be dodged,
Reluctantly he came to his true self.
How can a Christian soul be natural?

*The deposed Archbishop Cranmer, one of the founders of the Church of
England, main architect of the Book of Common Prayer, was burnt at the
stake at the instance of the Roman Catholic Queen Mary, successor to the
Protestant Edward VI, in March 1556, at the age of 67. His heresy was*

paradoxically to insist that the sovereign (Mary at that time) is Head of the Church of England. Mary owed allegiance to the Pope. In the last three years of Mary's reign, 1555–58, 300 Protestants were burned. Cranmer was forced to watch the burning of his old friends and colleagues Ridley and Latimer in 1555. All three were Cambridge dons who had preached Reformation doctrines in the Cambridge church, St Edward's, and used to meet for discussions in the Eagle Hotel in Bene't Street nearby. Cranmer, when imprisoned by Mary and her advisers such as Bishops Bonner and Pole, was brought to write a series of progressively more humiliating recantations, but they did not procure him pardon. Had they done so the course of English history might well have been different. But Mary and her advisers were determined to burn Cranmer. When they brought him to the stake in Oxford where Martyrs' Memorial now stands, to proclaim in public his humiliation, bringing the text with him, he also brought another text, recanting his recantations, which to general surprise, and at last acclaim, he then read, having now nothing to lose.

A traditional etymology for the name 'Mary' was 'bitterness'.

The Order of Dominican Friars, named after St Dominic their founder, were the most generally intellectual and theological of the various Orders of Friars. They were chiefly responsible for the Inquisition and were sometimes known by a pun on their Latin name as 'the hounds of God', Domini canes.

I owe part of the image of the 'rubber box' in which we find ourselves to a book by Mr Don Cupitt.

1994

THE SNAKE AND
THE LIZARD

We were walking the stony path up
The hill to the ruined village, through pines
When we saw them, snake and lizard,
Each ten inches long, with long jaws
Comically, horribly, overlapping and
Interlocked. How the snake wound his (her?) tail
Round the lizard to break her (his?) back.
How grimly the lizard locked immovable jaws,
And held rigid persistence. What
An argument. What insoluble question,
What impossibility of result. The wood
Was hushed, like us, expectant,
Shaded in brown, green and black, upon stone.
The snake thrashed.
The lizard bit hard.
Who would win? What need was at stake?
Why did they fight? What issue of prey,
Contest of territory could unite in enmity?
What righteousness in each, what anger?
Then they saw us, superior beings standing
High above the fight. They broke off
And scuttled away: no victor, no vanquished,
    nothing decided
No absolute truth of victory achieved
But at least a cease-fire had taken place,
Discretion's triumph over valour.

(This scene was observed in a wood on a hillside in Tuscany.)

Their hearts burned
within them.

EASTER DAY

THE FIRST EASTER DAY

THE WOMEN: 'It was the emptiness that frightened us,
The expected cold comfort of the corpse, gone.
Vacancy was full of threat, uncertainty.
No closure, nothing to embalm; the tomb
Hummed with silence. We had come to mourn,
But there was nothing; which meant anything.

We sought endurance of the loss, to heal
Or to embalm the absence; to preserve
Remains; to plug the gap with cloths, with oil.
So possession drains away, but slowly: at last
The bowl is empty but we hardly know
Until we need to wash the dishes or the feet
Of others, and find no being there to use.
Then loss itself is known, which is some gain.
We found a total absence of that loss
Which might have meant less human pain.
We ran away: we had nothing to say.'

MARY: 'Cruel! To have no well-known body there
To mourn, to clean, anoint, as when
He sat upon my lap. No turning to
Our general mother, earth, to let me think

Of days once joyful, bury them, and mourn
That strange imperious man, my son.
Where no body is, absence and loss have
Nowhere to lay their heads but wander through
The mind as restless ghosts, creating fear,
No joy returning. Rough soldiers were about,
And some young man said something
        I could not
Understand about being risen. But oh where
Is my son's body, plant of all my joy?
Lost, lost, never to be seen by me again.'

    Did the women talk?
    Did they run, not walk?
    There was no need.
    Done was the deed.
    The deed was done
    By the rising Son.
    A blinding light
    Destroys our sight.

You cannot stop Creation's way, to groan
In travail, then to flower and die: no pause
Even for God to contemplate. This is why
True beauty cannot last. The beauty lies
In its very passing, as it shifts our view,
As sun at dawn or sunset, as girls turn
Into wrinkled women. And so the suffering
Also cannot last. It self-destructs.
To hold the precious moment, as a drop of dew
May sparkle and disperse, is all our hope.

All we should seek. The dewdrop carbonized
As diamond combusts its beauty into death.

The walk to Emmaus

The ordinariness of places is
No guide to wonders that may happen there.
It was a common road to Emmaus
Something, like nothing, happens anywhere.

THE TWO
DISCIPLES:
'Who knows where the lightning flash will fall?
It tears the air: leaves on the retina a blaze,
A memory, a fear, which all have known.
But the memory fades. Yet it will come again,
Impossible to foretell. Why there? Why then?
A moment, all was clear, though after, black.
The brightness made the darkness visible.
Our hearts burned bright within us, shone
        out clear.
We turned and told, but what we understood
We never could explain. That evening walk
Has changed the world for us, has changed
        the world.
Why us, mere earnest ordinary men?
Why not his mother or some men of note?
We lived our later lives so justified,
But puzzled, unremarked, and yet redeemed.'

The ripened seed explodes and scatters as
The wind disposes and the earth receives;
Roots deep or shallow, fails, or multiplies

Brings fear, new life, flowers red as blood
    or death,
To grow, be cut as grass (immortal plant)
To rot again, to be consumed and live.
The sun must rise because it sets, and set
Because it rises. Is there then no rest?
Must all death only lead to life renewed?
If so, then fear is justified of new
Return, more effort to support the pain,
More effort to combat the ill, which is
Itself no more than ever-blooming life.
An end must be. Annihilation is our peace.

If greatest joy is cease of pain, so death
May be most joyful if the torture
Is most dire, so long as death's the end.
Destruction is creation's destiny,
God's goodness to be good itself must cease,
For goodness casts the shadow of the bad.
Where can we turn to escape the deep unreason
Of being here, save in the not-to-be?
Why act or suffer to maintain the good,
Since good brings bad beyond our reason's
    guide?
We float like flies upon the darkening stream,
Whichever way we dart the stream prevails.
We never can escape; at last we drown.
And nothing matters: it did not before.

A group of anxious men, devoted women
Heard rumours, explanations, some saw him.

73

More than they hoped, more than they wanted,
The solid visions came and went,
The categorical imperative
Was flesh and blood it seemed, which gave
    new sense,
Turning and twisting, what you will, yet not
At all to be expected, but be feared,
With utmost trembling arbitrary joy.

He had been one with all the springing growth
That struggles underneath the groaning soil,
Complexity of thrust that bursts into
The uncertain light, the treacherous
    changing air,
The intertangled contradictory powers
Which from the dark explode in colour like
A fire-work in the night, the messenger
Of devious destructiveness that makes
All life seek life and fall in fragments free.

The wind blows where it will
And never can be still.
The flame is always fanned
At some place in the land,
But not where you expect.
Presumption here is checked.
Only there's hope of fire,
Unsatisfied desire
For unrecorded joy,
For life without alloy.
The green tree may ignite,

The dry may suck delight,
The unknown find reward,
Mere justice be ignored.
No science here avails,
No general rule prevails,
But faith and hope and love
Down here and not above.

1989

THE DIFFERENCE

Sea coasts,
Rock and water
Hard and soft,
Tears and laughter.

Distinct seem life
And death, but sand,
Even storms, and bays
Confuse sea and land.

Merge is the word
As wind tosses hair:
Both sun and rain blind:
Let us all share.

Still night's not day,
Still we must die.
Things differ
Though clouds hide the sky.

By shutting my eyes
In a dull meeting
Fantasies rise
Of new happy greeting.

By shutting my eyes
There's no call to weep
At folly of the wise
Because I'm asleep.

PARANOIAC

Intensity of life will drive him on,
The passionate conviction that he's right.
The muttered word burst through clenched teeth,
The concentration of the circles of desire
Upon the single point and then the next.
The disregard for others and the need
For opposition from them makes
By paradox some others join the band
Of followers of his solitary need,
The paranoiacs bundled like the sticks
Of fable; soon he will unbind and cast
Them in the fire of disapproval which
He tends for all who disagree until
Consumed himself in his own darkened smoke.

ANCESTORS

The mad old King of the North shouted 'Bring down
The Stone Men our ancestors to join our banquet'.
His men went up to the misty hills to call
The grave stone men, incised with virtues
They had never possessed, and offered carts
But they proudly stumped down no one knew how,
Stood silent round the walls. Beer and wine flowed,
They heard the bold songs, listened to the boasts,
Unwearied, unblinking, as if were unknown
What all knew from the past and foresaw,
The quarrels, the brave men falling, the cowards.
As dawn closed eyes that should open they fell,
The stone men, on the feasters, crushed their bones,
Then marched stolidly back, an extra one with them
The King himself, stonily proud, stiff and grey,
And cold, inscribed with glory and defeat.

The Devil, as a roaring lion, walketh about,
seeking whom he may devour.

DEVOURING THE GOD

I

OLD TESTAMENT

EVE: God walked in our garden in the evening cool.
He saw the precious fruit had gone. I made Adam
Hide in the bushes. God looked different.
The apple rumbled in my belly and
I felt excited – saw Adam did so, too.
And God surprised me. He was not pleased, of course.
It seemed that time, which had stayed still before,
Passed like a cold wind through warm Paradise
And shrivelled him, but had engendered in me,
So I was big with knowledge even of God,
I knew him but he did not now know me,
He had diminished and I'd taken from him,
I had absorbed his power and mastery,
Which Adam might take from me: God would not.
He had become our Daddy, old and cross.

ADAM: I felt frightened, limp, too big, and self-aware,
Embarrassingly naked; so was Eve.
I wanted God to go away so that
We could enjoy ourselves in private. Shame
Self-consciously constrained us. God called, so we,

Came out, absurdly shielding private parts
Which, before time, we had not known as public,
Pubic, with cupped hands, until God told us how
To hide our private shame with public dress.
We thought ourselves as gods, equal to God,
Participating in divinity
With power, knowledge, hidden qualities.

The flaming sword drove us from Eden's wholeness,
Divided unity in labouring life,
Of toil, of art, of science, thought and death.
But ah, the joy of alternating change,
Pursuit of detail in its various wealth
Discovery of multiplicity,
Although we paid with sorrow for our gain
We counted then the world well won with pain.

II

NEW TESTAMENT

The bitter drink we brew and need is God
Himself; God's suffering sucked into ourselves,
God's own creative unregarded love.
We're drunken with our own divinity.
We drive the earth machine we have not made
Faster and faster through the universe
From which we have devoured, absorbed, used up,
Denied the god who fills us and who now
Cannot be tasted, known, seen heard nor felt.
Because it is ourselves who are as God,

We answer to ourselves alone, alone.
The black infinitude of empty space,
Drained of all meaning, value, merely there
As something not ourselves which pointlessly
Will roll on endlessly when we as gods,
Like God, ends in ourselves, will end in death,
Because we have devoured our God, become
Like gods, intoxicated with divine
Afflatus which must burst our mortal frame.

III

THE AFTERMATH

ADAM: Love is my drink and love is God.
I will swallow down love and love will control me
    with divine madness.
I am filled with love and madness.
I dance in an ecstasy, whirling on myself.
Dancing and whirling I am held upright
    by the drunken love within me,
Until at last the great weariness
The great sickness overwhelm me.
I spew up all my love,
I reel and shake, the world shudders,
Cold waves and hot go through my flesh
And I am my emptied sickened self.
The pain of the world is the pain of my body.
Nowhere is lucidity but stabs of light
That lighten no darkness.
There is no more love, no more meaning,

There is only emptiness within and mindless
    solidity without,
And only some shadows and gentler fires
Flicker between me and the null and blockish world,
To give some warmth, to make the bond that holds
    me to myself.
Inside and outside are different and the self
Must find and cling to the other not-self,
And I can never swallow God, he must remain
    outside me,
For within he will explode and destroy me,
As the cross exploded the dragon that wanted to
    eat Margaret
And Margaret can only keep the cross
When it stays outside, weighing her down,
Blockish, wooden, unspeaking, though known in
    the mind,
Quite inedible but real; and reality
Feeds the self as the self feeds reality.

IV

AND FINALLY ...

Inasmuch as you do this to me
You do it to others. See
The loafer in the wafer, the lady
As sweet as watered wine and free,

Though not perhaps so pure.
Then are you sure

You can avoid the lure?
Avoid yet love the whore?

You must show much, not
Too much love; but
Who can love a lot
Of scabs, funnies, wrinklies, but a nut?

Only God seems prepared
To take second best and dared
To be himself a nut, though scared
To be chewed as a kernel bared.

We find nourishment
Where he found punishment
We look for ravishment
Not banishment.

He is the God we eat,
The primitive meat,
The cosmic teat.
What do we excrete?

And to what lasting end?
Why did he send
His self-son to mend
The work of the fiend?

Why start it at all?
Why should there be a Fall

So we should also drink the gall
Of death's unavoidable call?

The swallows swoop and die
Though carelessly they fly.
Neither truth nor lie
Can tell them or us why.

They care not, nor fear
That death is near.
Ignorance is dear.
Their lives are clear.

But we must drink
And never think
From that bitter brink
To shrink.

Against our will we devour
The unsavoury sour,
The food divine, when the hour
To become ourselves a god is here.

What we eat is our fate,
Is the surrogate
To which we must relate,
Learning love not hate.

It was related in medieval story of St Margaret of Antioch, martyred in the early fourth century, that she, carrying a cross, was swallowed by a dragon who consequently exploded.

* 1988

EPITAPHS

I

Behind him he left a turbulent wake
Of gloves and pyjamas, his passport and tickets,
Forgotten appointments, his reading glasses
And once all his lecture notes. And all this apart
From what he more or less deliberately
Discarded, or preferred to forget. Then
He forgot and dropped, gasping and sinking, himself.

II

He was as if a pool ice-covered,
With boiling water underneath.
Not natural, you say; and he was not.
The water seeped away, ice cracked,
Fell into emptiness: the steam escaped.

III

Here lies one whose only merit
Lay in his total lack of spirit.
Nothing to give, nothing to say,
His body buried, clay to clay.

VI

Another here, did neither good nor harm
He served to keep some seats for others warm.

Reflect upon him as you pass him by,
He must alone in death as life here lie,
And you too, when your busy life is done
However loved and friended lie alone.

V

De mortuis nihil nisi bonum

This man was useless, timid, mean and rude.
Then say no more. At least for worms he's good.

VI

What is virtue, saith my sufferings then?

He found virtue hard as a mountain to climb,
Not being fit, not willing, no faith in the beauty
Of the view, and any way it was cold and misty
On the track, company few, not witty nor bright,
The path shown by stones and bones, wailing birds,
But he felt impelled, which was hardly virtue.

FROM THE TYROL

I

ON DESIRE FOR A CHANGE

Upon the flank
Of stony peaks
The snow lies blank,
Yet something seeks.

It will not rest,
It flows away,
With tumbling zest,
In melting May,

Its whiteness lost.
A turbid stream,
Steep downward tossed,
It breaks its dream,

Comes now to life,
The world to see,
And welcomes strife
Or amity.

From broken rocks
And darkening trees,
From swirls and shocks,
It then seeks ease.

The heavy river
Draws its bound,
Its own self-giver;
Ease is found

And torment lost,
Its own self so,
And painful cost:
Crowded low.

But lower yet,
The restless sea;
Ease to forget:
It now is free.
Eternity.

II

Haymaker's Song

The slope is steep,
The grass is long,
The scythe must sweep,
My arm is strong.

You come no more
With steady pace,
Who once before,
With blushing face

The flowery grass
Had helped to rake,
High up the pass,
For winter's sake.

The cut grass flowers
Each summer new
With freshening powers:
Not you! Not you!

Consequently I rejoice, having to construct something
Upon which to rejoice

FEAR AND TREMBLING

The first Isaac speaks:
  'So I learnt that God
  Is dangerous, a trusted
  Untrustworthiness. Things
  To come are still unsure,
  Providence is the past.

  With the young men
  I followed my father
  Over the unquestioned plain
  To the queries of the stony   10
  Blue mountains.

  Why had Mother not come?
  The last journey of childhood,
  Trust as assumed knowledge,
  Unbroken, where goodness
  Followed always in the green valleys.

  Like a walking sapling
  I followed my father,
  Like a mule I followed,
  Carrying the wood,   20
  Like myself I went
  Seeking the sacrifice.

But you must ask to know,
And knowledge may cut
The throat of him
Who seeks it. I screamed,
As goodness rose to kill.

The old blue eyes flared
Above me, the sky behind,
The same God's blue;   30
His wild hair astray like cloud,
The lightning-knife poised.

My spirit poured out
Like water, hardly was blood
Wanted as I saw
I was the sacrifice
To make evil dissolve in good.

Beneath me the rough sticks
Hurt my back, hostility
Of earth as of heaven   40
Would crush me between them.
And is it I who survive?

A flame burst from the sky
Lightning dashed lightning away
The ram struggled on my pyre,
Gushed red, was consumed.
My childhood burnt away.

How could I look at the old man?
His trembling hands undid my bonds
Rejoicing he kissed me lest I be angry,   50
We knew some new truth, but never now
Without question.

Never again to trust,
Always to fear,
Never firm and sure,
Always to shake.
The world a bundle
Of sticks to lie on.
Infinitude above.

Nothing is sure   60
Though the end certain.
The knife always there
To descend from the blue
Yet held in the blinding fire
Of its own intent,
Which may come when called
Or postpone its own fulfilment
Too give us space not peace,
To grow and flourish and wither
And burn and be taken up.'   70

The second Isaac came:
This time they nailed him to the wood.
They nailed him and he could not move.
God said to God, 'Why have you forsaken me?'
God said to God, 'I am terrible and weak.

I made the seas, forests, skies, fields, deserts,
Food and drink and the need for death.
But if you are travelling barefoot over the
   burning sands
And your tongue chokes you for thirst
I cannot cushion one footfall, give one cold drop   80
To comfort you. I am the beauty and the horror.
I am infinitely great and far away
And a still small voice within you.'

And the sky was cleft and the knife descended.
No ram was there to suffer for the lamb,
No other scapegoat but he
And fear must be felt as the cup is offered
And the cup of suffering is drunk,
And the cup of unfeeling declined,
And knowledge of all becomes dead to all,   90
And strength and weakness become the same,
Are terrible and holy, and the beginning
Of wisdom is fear.

So he was consumed and taken up,
And so must we be all,
And the end of our space is peace,
And with due caution we may
Rejoice in our trembling.

* 1979

SCHOLARS

In solitary untidy rooms we toil
(Though some think it not *work* but trivial play)
To trace in sedentary pursuit the wild
Lament, the racing heart, the anguished thought
Inscribed obscurely in a copy of
A copy, trapped in dusty books, of men
Who lived, and lusted, perished, long ago.
We read each others' solemn nonsense, even
Now send it through the air to flickering machines.
Not many care now what those past men thought,
Their similar or different joys and pains.
But we try still to get their words quite right.
We crawl down ancient passage-ways of mind,
Retrieve old lamps and burnish them anew
Illuminate some long lost thought or find
Some feeling now forgot and recognise
Ourselves and stare surprised at what we see.
We seek and lay old brick upon old brick
Of outworn knowledge, mortaring them anew,
Creating fakes more genuine than their ruins,
New fictions for the old to meet our new desires.
Within the half-glimpsed rooms of earlier time
We wait for inner light, the sudden spark
One thought flints off another, sudden flame.
All disappears within the light that blinds.
And in this light and heat we hear a voice
Commands and questions us, then leaves us cold,
To write again within the dull daylight,
Or under naked bulb of night, to tell,

With trouble what we think we heard and felt
To those few who attend to truth lit new.
But we have seen the light within our room
From ancient days, have felt the heat,
Have know communion with a mind like ours,
We are not all alone, not all astray.

IN THE LIBRARY

I

Deposited silt of meditative
And impassioned minds, new prejudice
Grown old and dry; even the dung
Of earlier thought reeks less, may fertilise,
Between old greasy calf or browning modern
Paper, all fallen here. Disorderly
And discontented rank beside all those
Who only regulated others' rot,
Now dust within dust, rarely blown over,
Both seed and soil for newer minds to work.

II

The old textual scholar looks at the girl on the other side
    of the table:
        Not much of my life
        Is left for disposal
        Too much is rife
        With earlier dispersal.

        Of what I control
        Some I would give you.
        Not much is central,
        A margin must do.

III

The girl thinks:
>I wonder what that old man does
>Hemmed in with books, his face as pale
>As parchment pages. Eagerly
>He looks from line to line, makes notes,
>Looks up and through me with a vacant eye.
>Is he a famous scholar? I do not care.
>I wonder what Jim's doing now,
>And most I wonder what this book can mean.
>How shall I learn the key to life?
>And shall I get that skirt from M and S?
>I wish I knew the author of this book
>To tell him how I love his crit of Yeats.
>And now it's coffee-time; I'll meet with Hugh.

IV

>And some there be of uneventful life
>Have fought some bloody battles of the mind
>Crouched paranoid in tangled prose,
>Crept down syntactic devious paths to spring
>With triumph and unsleeping sword upon
>Some errant critic dozing in the sun
>Of self-regard, discipleship or worse.
>Intensity of life! Unmeasured by
>The lust or greed or danger of the flesh,
>Unnoticed by the taxman or the Secretary
>Of Patronage! Its name lives evermore.

We are the circumcision who
worship by the Spirit of God

THE CIRCUMCISION

THE BIRTH

Divinity self-generated lights
The burning sun within the dark.
Its light bursts forth to make the shade,
The shadow-substance of the feeling flesh,
Constriction must precede year's needed spring.
Released he bounds to find the bounds he needs
For definition of divinity
And screams to find that joy must be confined,
Be bound and tied; then tried and guilty found.

On the eighth day.   10

The bloody rose now blooms between his legs
Pain flourishing for purity and love;
The infant scream prophetically begs
The non-existent mercy from above,
Foresees the executioner who pegs
The humanly divine with savage shove.

Blood and anguished urination,
Childish cries, archaic ritual of pain
Inflicted on that sweetest spur of life,
To mingle blood and water now as then.   20

What scandal to the Greeks; a whole hill
Of foreskins as a stumbling block
Grotesque in Rabelaisian multitude.
Our rationality such deity must wrack
That could redeem demeaned by such a lack.

Make holy, as the flint carves quivering flesh
The tenderest member, even as we are one.
Now have our eyes seen what salvation means
– Subjection to the custom of the tribe
Which customarily will reject their best   30
Who learn that custom undergone is overpassed,
And solitude must lead the way to light.
And with such light we go into the dark.

                To come to an end,
A Hebrew of the Hebrews, the torn flesh
Will doubly witness, first and last. The eighth
Day marked the entrance, and the end
Will mark us all as victims in the flesh.
Whatever rite or loss of rite or right we gain,
Ourselves must sink into the rotting flesh,   40
Be overwhelmed within that primal flood
Of darkness in the unknown lack of air,
Clutching the bloody wood that floats nearby
Which helps – or not – to rise up when we die.

Where are we? On whose side? Whom do we serve?
Direction fails in utter space, or none.
A lost rite, a lost right, leaves us cold,
Uncloaked, but suited, fore-warned and foreskinned.

Selfconsciousness our guide, who claims to know,
Leads us, detached from skin, from blood, to go   50
From dark to dark, to shudder from the knife,
Yet find a wounded nothingness in life.
We too may be of circumcision yet,
And losing confidence may still be met.

Circumcision amongst the Jews of Old Testament times was ceremoniously carried out on all male children on the eighth day after birth using a flint knife. It was the characteristic identification of the male Jew. St Paul also regarded it as a symbol of the crucifixion and in Philippians III, from which the motto is taken, further presents it in a metaphorical sense as characterising all believers and the power of resurrection.

* 1986

FROM THE BESTIARY
(EARLY THIRTEENTH-CENTURY ENGLISH)

I

THE FOX

There's a wild creature, full of wicked tricks,
Called a fox, cursed by farmers.
Both cock and hen
She takes to her den,
The gander and the goose
By neck and by nose.
Flesh and fowl fear and condemn her.
Listen now to a wonder that this liar does for hunger.
Goes to a furrow in a field, falls down in it,
Where ploughed or dug, to plot and deceive:
Doesn't stir more than stone, stays all the day,
Dead as a doornail, doesn't draw a breath.
The raven is very ready, and thinks that she rots,
And other flighty ones flutter down to find their food,
Daringly without distrust, thinking that she's dead.
They scratch this fox's skin – then she skips up,
Turns sharply on them, tickles them in turn,
Pays her bill
With ill-will,
Tears them to tatters with her sharp teeth,
Eats her fill,
And goes where she will.

II

TUSCAN HILLS IN SUMMER

'Backed like a whale'

These wooded hills sprawl out
Peaceful earth monster, floating in sky,
His shaggy sides unscarred, offering refuge
To fecund buzzing creeping walking lives.
And we are landed on him: let us not,
By lighting fires or other tricks cause him,
Antediluvian earth-whale,
To wake up angry and sink,
To drown us in circumambient blue air.

The Medieval Bestiary thought of the whale floating in the sea as like an island which sailors might land on.

EACH AS BAD AS THE OTHER

(From British Museum MS Harley 2253)

In fields in May at early light
The sounds arise of dear delight
Where leaves rejoice on tree.
Blossoms spread upon the boughs,
All nature sounds with sweet love vows,
As I so well can see.
But I know none such noble flower
As ladies bright within their bower
Who may with love be caught.
Of all such women in the West,
There's one of them I praise as best,
From India to Connaught.

Women would be the finest thing
Created by high heaven's King,
If many did not cheat.
But she's too ready in desire
To love who's latest to require,
When she should have her mate.
Those worth our faith in life are few;
Though ne'er to them we be untrue,
They're eager to betray.
And if love's promised with deceit,
He'll soon betray his lady sweet,
Whate'er his vows may say.

TAKE ME OR LEAVE ME

(ULC Ff VI 54 *f118v*)

Madame withouten many woordes
Mak me now siker, that ye wil or no;
And if ye wil thanne leve youre boordes
And use youre Will; nowe shewe me so,
For with a bek ye shal me calle.
And if of oon that brennes aye
Ye wil han pitė or routhe at alle
Answere hym feyre with ye or naye.
If it be ye, y shal be fayne.
If it be naye, freendes as before.
Another man shul yow attayne
And y myne owne, and youres nomore.

(By a follower of Chaucer: of unknown date. Not printed before.)

siker: certain
boordes: jokes
bek: beckoning
brennes: burns
ye: yes
y: I
fayne: glad

CONVERSATION OVERHEARD

He: I am a fool to love you, but my folly
      Dare not proceed to think that you love me.

She: Your folly is your wisdom if it knows
      That no excess is key to man's success.

He: Then as you are my folly, be my wisdom too.

She: But one thing cannot be the other and be true.

BY THE SEA-TIDE

'I love you' someone scrawls on the sands,
Committing himself till the next tide,
Which is long enough for holding hands.
But no. Reverse Nature's decaying slide.
Scratch it on rock and let the crashing wave
Smother it with foam or deeper surge, encrust
With shell and weed, hide in some darkening cave.
Once said it stays; though the writer may not.

Une belle chambre pour y mourir

AT THE GRAVESIDE OF
SIMONE WEIL

As I stand here amongst these ugly graves
I sometimes envy those who wish to die,
Who seek annihilation's mindless peace,
Lost in the mind of absent deity,
An absent-minded deity, forgetting
Those whom he created by his absence
Free, to yearn and struggle till exhaustion drowns.
So in the end you found some happiness
In finding nothing.
                                   It was fitting that,   10
So French, you died on alien soil; the priest
Forgot or missed his train; that you who could
Not take the Host or cross the church's sill
Should be consigned by an unconsecrated man,
For all was paradox and contradiction,
And they alone give hope that somewhere else
An overarching reconciliation
Must certainly exist – I don't know why.
The greater is the mind, the greater then
The contradictions held in play.   20
God's mind must needs be great to hold our world.

You sought perfection and that cannot be.
Poor Manichaean, through your love, not hate,
You saw that only that eternal dome

Of Blankness could be perfect, which is death.
Your brilliant intellect, that light divine,
Threw shadows blacker than the light could bear.
Then all the spectrum's mediating range
Denied leaves nothing but a nightmare blank.

The teeming hierarchies of the body-mind 30
The infinite riches in the little room
Within our skulls, and 'all the mighty world
Of eye and ear' you might acknowledge but
Transcended, reaching to that greater void
Beyond the void that rightly terrified
Pascal and makes me sick with dizziness
And beauty. But transcendence only means
The loss without redemption, mere deceit
Of self: all value, justice, love, denied.
It terrifies beyond the fear of Hell. 40

Contempt would be all that you'd feel for me;
My compromise with comfort; use and yield
To force; my love of all that should accompany
Old age, as honour, troops of friends, and sense
Of work well done which in your eyes was not
Worth doing; my lack of certainty; my fear
Of death; my need, from weakness, to forget
The misery and slavery of the poor
Which would not let you be; my need for
Firm attachments though you recognised 50
The need for roots – but I need movement too.
The relative and not the absolute
Is what we need and gladly will make love

Not only to the virgin but the whore.
The mistress absolute is out of reach
Of average sensual stupid men like me.

The terrible beauty of your daily life
Shines through the dowdy clothes, the cigarette
   burns,
A fierce truth like the blazing forges where
You worked which scorched you to the soul. You lost 60
Your gaiety for ever in that burning
Fiery furnace. No stranger joined you.
Fraternity, like God, was known by absence;
Equality was known through loss of rights,
And Liberty was freedom from the self.

You wrote as with a pickaxe to break through
That egocentric shell, the world perceived,
To find, with words, the silent emptiness
Made by the blessed abstinence of God,
The self beyond the self which is no other   70
Self, which rests on the impossibility
Of self knowing self in depths of being,
And in that ignorance finding space for grace.

Like moth to candle-flame you came to God
And were destroyed. And so my mind returns
To you, repelled, compelled. The guttering flame
Burns on, not for itself, but for us all.
The light and shadows leap within our cave.
The moth learns beauty, truth, affliction, all   80
Are one in immolation of its self.

The flame burns on, immortal justice lives:
The flame consumes itself, becomes a void,
Leaving its vivid absence stamped on air.
In darkness flame and moth are one, and none.

Analogy breaks down, words fail. Renew
The effort.
            For you I claim what you would not,
Courage and love, to think unthinkable thoughts
To love the unlovable (only you would not love   90
Yourself). Intensity and purity
Of soul, piercing the common shell of life
Yet honouring it while breaking. Tenderness
And bitterness both filled the cup you emptied:
You found within the emptiness a grace
That passes understanding in its weight.

You punished your own body hoping thus
To mitigate the pain of other's pain.
Hating the pain of others and yourself,
Hardship and danger were your spirit's need   100
Like men exploring desert wilderness
Or questing knights who sought they knew not what
But found their sin, and wounds, and solitude,
Then comfort of society when they
Returned, which you abolished for yourself
For you would not say 'we'.
                        Heroic soul,
Denying all the claims of body's clay,
Accepting it for decreation's sake,
The pot being fired, its use to hold a void,   110

Then found a waster from excess of heat
Fit only to be thrown away, your spirit
Had no vessel in this world, and fled.

(Simone Weil (1909–43) French philosopher, mystic, ascetic, of Jewish family, attracted to but not joining the Roman Catholic Church, spent her last year working with the French Resistance in London. She died of starvation, unable to bring herself to eat while so many victims of the war were suffering. Among her works are La Pesanteur et la Grace *(1947, translated as* Gravity and Grace, *1952) and* L'Enracinement *(1949, translated as* The Need for Roots, *1952).)*

1987

COLLEGE CONVERSATION LATE SIXTIES

'I'm glad to see you Peter: how's the work?'
'Not good. As yet I'm not prepared. I need
To know first who I am, and where I stand
On fundamental principles, to clear
My mind, get right priorities, sort out
Directions, and establish proper values.
Until then, how can I settle to discern
The ultimate significance to me,
The relevance, of those whose only claim
To my attention is that many men now dead
Have thought them good? Originality
Is what I look for.'
                'Peter, death stands waiting
At your shoulder, as at mine: Will you
Be ready then? Is that original?'

ME AND NOT ME

O my subconscious is an ill-trained dog
Who bounces on uncertain leash, not much
To do with me except he's mine,
More vagrant, stupid even than am I.
He does not lead or tell me anything
But drags me through some unknown ways
Exciting or embarrassing or dull.

CARO'S METAL SCULPTURES

Is this our world?
Girders (we live in a girding age)
Tubes, tie-rods, leaning planes,
Thrusting, lifting, balanced
To make imagined fingers scream at
Angle, twist, crush, drop.
Furnace and fiery blade, no natural metaphor,
Forges pipes conjunction to circle,
Rivets to clasp, yet remain cold
As a farm-machine bright harrow in a gray field.
May-morning* is red pipes, alive in the mind,
They lean, enter, curl, spread, stiff, stop.
Hopscotch* static in leaping bars,
Witty, scattered to gather a point cool.
Sleepwalker* in delicate traverses of pipe
Leads up into air, nowhere.
Metal wound on to table tops,**
Poised curve to flat, green of enamel
Not grass, red-lead not blood;
Shaving mirror; climbing frame;
Fairground images, pounding pistons,
Workshop angulosities, dead steam-engines,
Precision-made, junk-yard litter,
All is here from Industrial Revolution
To the barren moon.
All is hard, firm, held up,
Tilted, balanced forceful not stable,

---

* refers to actual named pieces
** small pieces are 'table top sculptures'

Yet won't rock, won't sway in the wind.
Nor any false heroic; little ones
Perched on a table-edge, not edge
Of eternity; big ones for a field,
Too big for my town-garden. Gestures
Man-made, not personal, lifted they are,
Not seeking; unsought, unfeeling
Witty and blank as a rhomboid.

As flies to wanton boys
are we to the gods

JOB'S WIFE

JOB: I sit here on the midden.
      Who speaks to me? I sit here.
      Who speaks? Whose is the voice, voices, voiced void?
      Who am I now, that was a man, Job, owner of himself,
      Of others who told him who he was?
      Now who tells me what? I shut my eyes to the light.
      In darkness I sit, I (or is it I?) call.
      Who hears? Whose voice is that? Is there a voice?
      Do I speak? Who speaks? Who hears?

JOB'S   In another world, under a different sun   10
WIFE: I had children and natural goods.
      Now all are gone, are gone. I weep with Rachel.
      What fault was mine? I am the woman,
      Condemned to bear in pain, suckle in joy,
      Then lose, and weep, make no complaint.
      My children gone, breasts dry, belly slack,
      And you fail in your strength as man.
      No more will be begotten, yet you sit
      In idleness, you do not seek revenge.
      Revenge yourself on God, the unjust, who grants   20
      The Shaitan licence to deprive, torment us
      For a sport, a test. I will not play before him.
      All my precious children dead, all dead.
      The camels and the sheep, your treasure, friends,

Are nothing to my loss, which is yours too,
Your sons and daughters. Resist. Do not accept
The ignominy of resignation to the will
Of God whose will is arbitrary; no love, no good
At heart but only with the power to do
Or not to do, or licence others who   30
Will only harm.
   To worship God whose will
Is not to honour or protect you whom he made
Is in itself dishonourable. The only good
Is blasphemy, denial, to assert
Superior moral power. Curse God and die.

JOB: The mystery of God cannot be known
For us it is enough that we are here,
Must make in every sense the best of it,
Driven by forces that we can't control.   40
The whirlwind mocks us with its roar.
Yet out of it a still small voice may tell
Of hope and love and goodness in the end.

JOB'S You are proud in your patience, pity does not stir you.
WIFE: More moral than the Almighty, you move anger
     in me.
Where are the homes, where our hopes? Happiness
     dwindles to nothing.
All our wealth is our woe, weariness and darkness.
The sun burns us, storms rot, we sink into vacancy,
All's lost, your body loathesome, you linger on dung.
Identity is troublesome, torment alone marks it.   50

You rest without remonstrance, you receive
   without responding,
You accept your afflictions; you should assert
   your rights,
Curse God and die.

JOB: I cannot see the world without the Lord,
      Though good and evil, injustice, gladness, pain
      Incomprehensibly, offensively,
      Are mingled here for me alone to sort.
      The circuit of my mind, the rounded whole
      On which identity, perception rest,
      Is incomplete without the present Lord.   60
      Perhaps compulsion of his being himself
      Requires both me and Satan to exist
      To make the rounded whole of his own self.

JOB'S Because God abdicates responsibility
WIFE: Allows the Shaitan have his sport with us
      As cat plays with a mouse, not killing it,
      But making it a rag of fear and pain,
      Is that a reason for excusing him,
      Making precariousness of life a good,
      Seeking to know God who does not seek us?   70
      Why should we value what's no worth to him?
      The desert's strewn with bones; mountains hide
      The frozen corpses of a myriad tribes.
      Within the seas waver and rot millions
      Of corpses. Armies perish under God
      And generals, ordered to wasteful death
      By vanity, incompetence and greed.

Some men will fight for duty, loyalty,
Thinking it virtue to be brave for God
Who does not care; and many other men   80
Will fight because they love destruction or
Because they're told of loot or women at
Their will, or they themselves are bullied into war,
Or simply do not think at all. The world
Stinks high of useless ill-spent life and death.
Do not collaborate. Curse God and die.

Job: To curse God, then to die, is to give up.
I will not deny my own integrity.
I will sit on the dung, cover my head with ashes,
Admit that I may have made mistakes, been   90
Without due care as all men sometimes are.

You may cover my head to feet with boils,
Pour on my head fiery consolation
By old friends that I must have sinned,
By young men that I am self-righteous but
I will not deny my own integrity.

I did what I thought was best, gave to the poor,
I fasted twice a week, I was not proud,
I did my best to obey the commandments,
All these with such good will as God gave me.   100
I will not deny my own integrity.

Tell me of the power of God, above good and evil,
Let God unleash the dog of evil,
That he lick my disgusting sores. I will not blame God,

Nor will I be bullied and give in,
Nor will I deny my own integrity.

Let all my possessions, my loved ones, be destroyed,
My anguish, my unintended sins, be confirmed,
Let all the world be consumed in flood and flame,   110
Let my whole life be thought a failure
I will not deny my own integrity.

Torture me with what was, or might have been,
With injustice, or justice, or disregard,
With solitude, with company, heat or cold,
Let my body scream against me, let me die,
But I will not deny my own integrity.

This must be in the end what God wants,
That we hold on even when our children
Are torn from us, when we lose the fatherly love,   120
When the beloved wife reproaches us,
That we do not deny our own integrity.

Though God be truth, beyond God is a truth,
That some kind of love must be; and rest in death.
Uncertainty, not God, reigns here below.
His power is withdrawn, is guessed, so that
I may not deny my own integrity.

JOB'S The mighty works of the Lord praise him.
WIFE: The beauty of the hills, the sunlit shores praise him
        With the noises of joy, the peaceful smiles
           of content.   130

But how shall the cripples, the mothers of starving
    children,
The widows, the stupid, the orphans, praise him?
How shall the barren desert, the killing cold,
    praise him?
How shall those praise him who love others' pain
If their praise be not a scream of derision?
What praise can the greedy and mighty
Who inherit the earth give him that does not
    wound
A thousand times more those they have wronged?
Their praise, or their silence, are curses on God.

JOB: Satan is God's shadow, the dark against the bright.   140
They are one yet not one. They are
Within, above, below all good and evil,
The pounding heartbeat of the universe,
Systole against dyastole.
Who can question such power?
By patience we endure; by patience
We conquer, without power, and we assert
Our singular humanity.
The arbitrary will of the chequered Lord,
The power and the glory his alone.   150
Who can question it and his ways?
His love is not to be doubted.
For he wills us to live for a while,
Though we squeeze through gates of pain,
A little, little while, for our days and years.
Even a thousand years of our generations
Are to him as the brief moment of yesterday,

And our pain must become his, though still ours.
We are his children. He must suffer through us.   160

The little that we are that is our own
Is not within our own power to dispose.
We float as on a billowing sea, or as
Men wandering in a desert with no path.
We carry others' goods that may sustain
Our life, until their weight will drag us down
To rot among the unseen swirling depths
Or dry with other bones upon the sand.
Some time a scented wind will blow us fair,
Or we shall find green pastures by the way: 170
In either case no guiding mind of ours
Has led. A rod and staff may help, a mast
And rag of sail take up a prosperous wind,
But all is providence or fortune. None
Is ours. Listen then for voices in the air,
Or from the deep – from anywhere outside.

JOB'S   We were not there when God made all. We were
WIFE: Not asked. No answer comes to stay my cry.
        Prosperity may go and come. Let Job,
        Now tested, tried, resolved in faith, restored,   180
        Find under God more wives, more children, wealth.
        But nothing can bring back my children dead,
        And nothing will save suffering to come,
        My race and others, ever tormented.
        Of what use is the power that makes the storm,
        The mountains, sunny seas? Bring back to me
        The nameless women, followers of Eve,

The pain-born babes, more worth than all that world
Where Shaitan is licensed to rage and reign
Before the Lord, to make him sport, a test   190
Of his creation as it screams in travail.
The day will come when men have power like God,
Shall girdle the earth, move mountains, seas,
And pierce the heavens and speak to all the world,
And make the lakes like poisoned deserts, the air
To choke them as they breathe, the fields be barren.
To boast of power, men's power will be as God's,
And will as wantonly destroy, then die.

JOB: The power of God is not in nature's force
Or beauty. The mighty mountain or the storm,   200
'The sounding cataract' or 'the force that through
The green fuse' sends its fire through our blood,
Nor setting or the rising of the sun,
Or howling winds, or plains of fruitful grain.
The power at last lies in the still small voice
That is not power at all, but may control
The wavering minds of women and of men.

So I will live despite of evil and of pain,
Because they are not all. Purpose and the good
May still be found. Nor should prosperity   210
Be despised though transient, nor the happy end,
Though it be image of a certain death.
And so I praise what I can find to praise,
If only praise itself, against the odds,
For still uncertainties preserve our hopes,
And God, not Shaitan, is our first and last resort.

EPILOGUE

We cannot bring down God for justice or
Who would escape due punishment?
Mercy dances before him, tearing off
Her veils. He longs to see her stripped, pure   220
Naked truth, no wanton subterfuge
Of human disguise, that she may bring him
The head of reason, logic, the sacrifice
Of troubled death, the forerunner, prophet
Of reconciliation, sacrifice to stronger truth,
The freedom to choose inevitable death.
He is beyond us yet within us; he made us
We are not him, but we too must make him.
We lose ourselves, our wills, in him, yet
We must retain ourselves, sit stubborn on   230
Our dunghill selves, believe ourselves like him
Resist the devil, not collaborate.

Defiance or endurance, both are right,
But not enough. The question must be put,
And not to ask will leave us in the sludge
That generates no energy or love.
Why should we suffer, innocent? To ask
May not be meaningful: then we must be
Ourselves as god, and that way madness lies.
So ask again. Do not despair. For power   240
Is not enough. It must be crucified.

1995

SO WHAT

This strange interval between unknowing and forgetting,
Full of desires that vanish if fulfilled
Or pester us if unappeased, both uselessly,
We fill with earnest play and foolish sadness,
Inventing aims and purposes to hide
The emptiness of knowledge of oblivion.

So grasp the moment, or the lover, or rebuff.
If one escape, the other is still there,
And in the moment following another
Comes, or nothing, and time past is nothing.
We live between two nothingnesses still.
The moment only is alive, but that will pass.

IN CHURCH AT DUSK

These strong columns, arches, try to net
The blue absolute, draw it down to light
The dusty corners of our transient day.
The absolute slips through the heavy weave,
Drains out, to leave us dark and wondering.

CALIBAN AND HIS DOG

'You taught me language and my profit on't
Is, I know how to curse.'

If my dog could speak at all he'd say
'I love you, I love you, I love you; all
I want, I want, I want, is water, food
And sex, a lot of sleep, what fun, what fun,
Let's go together; love, I love', and so forth.
Which would be very boring not because
Unintellectual but so stable, constant,
And altogether too adoring. What
A good thing dogs are not blessed with speech.
Unfortunate am I that am so cursed,
Having only hatred to express.

Nothing is so delicate and
fugitive by its very nature
as a beginning

IN THE BEGINNING

I

The Death of Myth

In the beginning was chemical soup
As Oparin, Haldane, Bernal, Watson, Crick,
Bold scientists, say about the unfolding patterns
They invent, explore, and we must accept,
With purpose to explain the purposeless.
We burst the cramping framework of old myth
And spread and breathe in mind – not spirit – free;
That wilful potter moulding up his clay
To fire us in this agony of life
Fades in the daylight of our ordinary pain.   10
And best of all the hideous fantasies
Of earlier men unconscious of themselves
Shrivel to a lamentable joke as must
That primal eldest phallus of the sky
Which drenched promiscuous earth with fertile seed.
Pathetic sex-drenched ignorant speculations:
Like those of our poor ignorant Norfolk miners
Huddled in white sludge of pits where black
Voluptuously shaped flints must be picked out
With antlers only stronger than their fingers,   20

Scraping darkness from light, heavy with weak.
Productivity as usual the cry,
Invoking deity they shaped their earth-goddess
Ready to burst with life; nearby, two balls
(Of stone), a rod – earliest of incentives,
Technology's first tool, to magic out
The flints, in that ancient boring industry.
Silly sex-fantasy, mythic and false,
Only to be valued for the interest
With which, though false, it clothes the drudgery   30
Frustration, boredom and brutality
Of primitive lives and modern literature;
Our great achievement now to break its hold,
Divorce from value, turn sex to an itch,
A joke coagulating in the talk
Of business-men and London dinner-parties,
Americans, films, colour-supplements,
The frisky marginalia of our lives.

I do not like it but the truth seems so
And we must follow where it seems to go.   40

And so reduce all other myths that bind
Us to their framework. Nothing can be meant.
That primary soup itself is figured wind,
Another myth that scientists invent.
Beginnings are impossible. Behind
The First is always germ and precedent
As far as thought can stretch. Nothing the mind
Cannot conceive. Nor can the end be lent
A meaning. Bodies die but mouldering find

Loathesome continuity, different   50
Progression. Our inner minds may not survive,
But we can only think while still alive.

We think now in our personal circumstance,
While standing on this cold and windy corner.
Heaped flowers pass us by; within, the sheeted
Grinning nothingness that we shall be.
The easy image of the flowers and corpse
Muffles with significance the sense
That all we do, as accidents of time,
With no more history than our struggling lives,   60
Is to invent beginnings in a world
Where self-subsistent mindlessness rejects
Our very formulation of its lack
Of mind. Purposefully we perceive
No purpose. We judge that there will be
No judgement. We must keep the paradox.
Although there is no doubt the world exists,
It never did begin. No end will be
Because beginning has not been. We learn
With fear the open spaces of our freedom   70
Still cramped within the teleology
Of language that still fails to match our thought;
But we must teach ourselves now to rejoice.

II

SECULAR HYMN

Self-enclosed and systematic
Finite yet unbounded space
Is undirected and chaotic,
Mindless and without a face.

We must live with contradictions,
It is only we who judge;
We must invent our value-fictions   80
Till the last entropic sludge.

III

IN THE MIDST

And so we build on sands of endless time
Because we can find nothing else. And Patience
Sits with middle-age, hopes no storm will come.
Solutions that are Final are a crime.
It is the young, the truculent fearful young,
Who scrabble down to bedrock, tilt our house,
Reveal their naked fathers in their fear
And learn the empty spaces of the heart.
So start again, but do not seek beginning;   90
Jump into your present skin, this *now*,
Here at this point of time, on which all past
Converges in this subtle knot, or tangle,
Its strings connected infinitely for-
                                        Ward . . .

IV

A World Language

.... in the middle of a sentax
Among language circumambient but strange;
Known unknown characters we analyse
In deep complexity. Dawn and sunset now,
The meadow with its golden flower, the green   100
Surging seas of hills and waves, the snowy alp
Too simple for the questing mind that forces
Us beyond the air, within the molecule.
We solve the syntax of the world, we hold
Its powers as the fireman holds his hose.
To turn now where we will, their origin unknown,
An utterance with structure that develops
But has no end and therefore no beginning,
A pattern not a meaning: no main verb –
(Unless a metaphor of long ago   110
Be demythologised and keep its sense).

V

A Centre whose Circle is Everywhere

Look for the centre, mark it with a cross,
Which shows we would sign if we knew the word;
Stands for the word we cannot write or read;
– Would name us to ourselves and settle doubt,
Perhaps, – existed once as love and pain
Authoritative and without an end.

VI

Ending the Ending

The fireman's hose jets out the stream of life
Of which he is himself a part. No strife
Internal to the man, with men, or things,   120
Can break the continuity that brings
Our comfort in each other, in the world,
But also holds us chained in thought and hurled
With perishable matter to an end –
Say rather, change we cannot comprehend,
Supreme yet insignificant, unknown,
The pattern broken; is the meaning shown?
All words dissolved in meaning then perhaps
Made plain though personality may lapse,
For now syntactic complements of light   130
And dark may hint a meaning in the night
And knowledge of long-lasting love that we
Do not deserve, whose loss is agony,
And in that other agony, more undeserved,
That showed us how the world could be so served
That ending in itself can be transcended,
Apocalypse an aberration mended,
That men no longer need a curtain round
Their airless beds which set the nightmare's bound,
No longer need forbid the eternal sea   140
With myths of starting and catastrophe.

The universal meaning cannot be
Limited in time; it must be free
And men content to read it differently.
Interpreting needs love, not pedantry.

*The reference in section I is to the ancient flint mines in Norfolk now
called by their eighteenth-century nickname, Grimes Graves.*

* 1970

FAITHFUL LOVE

You could see he loved her by the way he looked
And she floated in admiration but was bored.
Setting her sails to catch a more exciting breeze,
She would tack against a stronger wind, lean
Dangerously over, show her dashing sides,
And plunge through a rainbow spray,
And longed to ride a storm, needing the risk,
Preferring, or so she thought, to wreck
Her hopes rather than have calm voyage,
And a solid grave. It wasn't so for him.
He always blew warm, he could not change.
But how dull for her, remorselessly
Beloved by one who had he found her becalmed
Could not have moved her. I sometimes wonder,
Would God be bored if we truly loved him
As he, they say, loves us? We are surely bored by him.
There's little chance, though, he'll be bored by us.

NORTHWARDS

(told by King Alfred)

He had met no land that was tilled
Since he left his own home:
But all the way on the side of his steering oar
Was the waste (hunters, fishers, fowlers,
Wandered sparsely in it between
The white mountains and the greedy grey-lipped sea):
And as he leant on the heavy oar
He kept his back always to the widening sea.
A cold journey, and getting colder,
In the warm time of the year,
When the early roses were red
In his own home further south.
As he swayed high in the stern,
And the strange sea mouthed his oar,
And the south wind pushed him slowly north,
Where men had never been before,
He searched with his pale eye
Not for Ultima Thule, but for the walrus,
Which has such fine bone in its teeth,
And he watched how the land bent back
(Or did the sea bend forward, biting its edge?
– He had no eye for scenery –)
And neither believed nor disbelieved
The stories he heard from the Permians,
When he reported to me, but did not recount them,
Not having seen for himself.

An unimaginative man, you say?
A calculating eye, a mind of clay?
Yet impulse more than wind had driven him north.
His blank mind searched for more than ivory's worth.

Ohthere, the subject of this, a Norwegian merchant and mariner (9th century), travelled north by sea round the top of Norway and down the coast of the White Sea. He reported back to King Alfred, who inserted an account, occasionally followed quite closely here, in his translation into Old English of the universal history written by Orosius in Latin.

And as an aungel hevenisshly she soong

THE SMALL SOUND OF A TRUMPET
(HILDEGARD OF BINGEN)

I

Nine hundred years ago
The inner flame was lit that burnt at last
Its shrivelled case to join the everlasting light
Whose sparks had lit you as its tinder to inflame
The dry bones lost in arid contemplation.
You are burnt up, become a nothingness
To reach God's all. Struggle no more.
Now love that fired you is both wick and flame,
Is consolation, glory and reward.
No need for fierceness; ashes now to ash,   10
The dust of self and conflict blown away
By the spirit's power of which in life you sang.

Your song still lives with us, beyond belief.
We hear the song you sang along the cloister garth,
To God and to yourself. Now both are gone
And light that lightened you in darkened cells
In days on earth is scientifically conned.

II

You felt the airy fire within your guts.
Within your head the circles whirled around

The stars, winged beasts flew by.   20
Your mind's intensity pierced orbs of light,
But unafraid, surprised by joy, at five years old,
Like any child you took what was for granted.
You saw strange light and felt no fear and spoke
Of it to no one, even kindly Jutta,
Devout and dull, who fostered you, shut up
Together, child and ageless nun, within
That tiny cell, space capsule for eternity.

Misfiring neurones sparked the engine of
Your brain, hurled fireworks like the 'light divine,   30
All lights excelling', multicoloured, bright,
Transcending all the world's dark sky of sin,
Beyond all space conceived by earthbound men.
Yet what of evil could you know? At last you sang
In praise of Blessed Mary and the saints.
Virginity released you from the bonds
Of flesh, of men, of vanity, of all
The matter, good and bad, that constitutes
The fallen world of lost perfection where
Virginity alone is Paradise.   40

Your songs sprang like fresh flowers to hymn that joy,
Virginity's intensity and power, celestial harmonies,
Self transforming self, forgetting self.
So small an instrument you felt, so thin a note,
Which yet has echoed down nine centuries
To minds ill-tuned to all you celebrated.
The voice from heaven spoke to you.
The sharp ears of your mind caught every sound

That chanted burning love, and image after image
Tumbled out, like falling rocks in waterfalls,   50
For you were showered with answers high enthroned
In lurid colours of another world
Not seen by other eyes, transformed to God.
At last you spoke and sang and wrote, revealed
The wonder of your mind.

III

Your mind ablaze with light shone fierce with love
That for itself to live must have its counterpart
Of earthy mixture of the dull and bad,
The necessary foundation of the ways you searched,
Which could not of itself bring forth the green   60
You loved, which only love could generate,
Hot love that rained sweet tears of joy and grief,
That drew upon the water of life from high,
Which then fed waters underneath the earth
To fertilise both tares and wheat and hope,
The circuit of redemption of the world.
If good exists then evil must do too,
Both products of the self-conflicted Word.

So self-contained, not anxiously, not clinging to
Your Daddy, when he made of you his tithe,   70
No longing for your mother, nor the nine
Preceding you at home, transferring love,
Eager to please your God, you sought and
        found him
Strangely pleased to pin you to your bed

With spears of pain, which then you turned against
Recalcitrant and holy men, who yielded
To your humble pride beyond their comprehension,
As decency yields to conviction's power.

IV

That you are filth and ash and lie in pain
Saves self-regard from wounding you. And no   80
Neurosis in you leads to self-contempt.
Acceptance of your nothingness, your lack
Of power, frees you for the exercise of will,
Gives confidence untroubled by the self,
The gift of nothing gives you all. Without
Will of your own you force us on your way.

V

'The living fountain' speaks through you, a force
That wells up from those waters under the earth,
Above the sky, that flood away all doubt,
The stagnant slimy pools of dull neglect.   90
You never doubted jewels should adorn your nuns,
For why should God disdain the glory that
Is made from his work polished by our own?
You knew high rank marked true nobility,
For has not God made all society?
You saw that sin is everywhere and pain,
And knew, or thought you knew them both within
Yourself; but being in yourself without
The self-esteem that holds men bound to earth

You floated as a feather on God's breath,   100
Or as a leaf upon his fertile stream.

VI

Fierce little woman, passionate to get your way.
Admonishing popes emperors abbots monks,
But rather not your way but God's as you
Would say and holy men believed. They quailed,
Though women sometimes could stand firm against
Your fulminations. The father spoke in you,
And daughters of the spirit found they could resist.
Richardis the beloved broke away,
And left you lonely. Yet you could drink   110
From when your will was crossed the bitter truth,
As sharp as love gone sour, that no one can be trusted,
Except for God, and he will send you trials,
A Comforter whose rod is heavy on your back,
But is the staying truth that you must kiss.
All human love must pass. The green leaves, flowers
You loved, must fade like music's cloistered notes.
Abandonment, betrayal are the tests,
The benefits that do not go away,
The painful vacancies that leave a space   120
For what will not abandon you, your love
For God, whose grace and sweetness overflows
At last the bitter cup you hold so firm.
You saw the glory of the Lord, the world;
Explained the causes, gave interpretation
As mouthpiece of the Lord with humble certainty.
The incandescent mental lava spread

Throughout the world you knew, congealed
Into a massed humility so humble
It hardened into selfless self-assertion   130
That still was hot with love for Heaven's world.

VII

But what is there for us here to believe?
Our comforts cushion us and deaden sense
With sensual mediocrity. We drowse
In sweetened coma. The pain of loss,
Acidity that bites on steel to grave
In our and other hearts new messages,
We neutralise. The dreaded shears come now
As comfortable hollow needles. We ask
No spears of brilliant everlastingness,   140
No flagellation of the body or mind,
Content to float above a meaningless
And arbitrary void, which justifies no rule,
No bravery nor sacrifice, condemns no crime,
Has purpose without purpose, only allows
Conspiracies of those who think alike,
And force their way for others' good or ill.
But you were different, a force yourself,
Yet confident it was not you alone
Who led the way to find the Promised Land.   150

Then death for you was joy, arrival, light,
Your self restored, fulfilled, and gathered up,
Returned into the Father's loving care.

The poem's 153 lines evoke the symbolism of the number 153 (that of the miraculous draught of fishes, John XXI, 11), traditionally the number of death, completeness, perfection and salvation, being the sum of all its component digits.

St Hildegard of Bingen 1098–1179, the tenth child of a noble family in Germany, was dedicated by her father as a 'tithe' offering to God at the age of eight to be totally enclosed at the Benedictine monastery at Disibodenberg, in the care of a nun called Jutta. From the age of five she had had visions, now regarded as the product of a rare form of migraine, which she regarded as divine, but did not disclose until she was about 38. At this time she became head of the convent of nuns. A few years later she began writing remarkable works, both devotional and scientific, based on her visions, or learned, in prose and verse. She wrote music to her rhapsodic words, songs which she herself sang. Her increasing fame attracted many recruits, and eventually she 'suddenly announced that she had received a command from God to remove her nuns to Rupertsberg' (Flanagan, p. 5), a proposal that was long strenuously resisted by the monks. After a long illness and much prayer she got her way. Soon after 1151 her favourite nun, Richardis, a daughter in her affection, was elected abbess of another convent and left her, to her great grief. Her health was often poor, especially when she was opposed, but her life was full of writings of remarkable power and originality (a sort of medieval female version, ceteris paribus, *of William Blake though he had none of her responsibilities and organisational achievements). Despite her physical frailness she travelled to some extent, and conducted a vigorous correspondence, whose recipients included the Pope and the Emperor. She also had a prolonged dispute towards the end of her life with the monks of Mainz. She died peacefully on 17 September 1179. (Details from Flanagan.)*

She wrote that the Church resounds like a trumpet in three ways, and that she too, spoke and sang as the voice of God, though she claimed that her trumpet note was but thin. Despite her apparently limited experience and education her literary, scientific, even medical, and musical achievements remain most impressive. Her range was wide, and despite her asceticism she valued beauty, both natural and man-made, as the gift of God.

See Hildegard of Bingen, Causae et Curae, *ed. P. Kaiser (Leipzig, 1903);* Scivias, *transl. Mother Columbia Hart and Jane Bishop, Introduced by Barbara Newman, Preface by Caroline Walker Bynum (New York and Mahwah: Paulist Press, 1990);* Symphonia, *ed. with Introduction, Translations and Commentary by Barbara Newman, Second Edition (Ithaca and London: Cornell University Press, 1998).* On Natural Philosophy and Medicine, Selections from Cause et cure, *ed. Margret Berger, Cambridge: D.S. Brewer, 1999.*

Dronke, Peter, Women Writers of the Middle Ages *(Cambridge: Cambridge University Press, 1984).*
Flanagan, Sabina, Hildegard of Bingen, 1098-1179, A Visionary Life *(London and New York: Routledge, 1989).*

1998

NAMING THE NAME

The name has power to speak but only to those
Who know the language, who believe that words
Are not mere self-denoting sounds but call
Upon us; but only call if we respond
With love and knowledge. D'you know my name?
Call me. Will I answer? Only if I know
Myself, have learnt my name, been taught
To know myself as such, and want to speak.
Do I know you? Shall I reveal myself?
And if I do will it surprise or make
You feel the lesser or the more than me?
To name myself will give myself to you.
To make a gift is to exert my power.
If you know me maybe you'll master me,
Or mistress me; I you – will that be good?
But first of all you must tell me your name.
I'll take your name and then
I'll number you.

(Note: Arthurian story makes much play of knowing, telling or not telling, a name. In the army for someone to have his or her 'name and number' taken is a necessary preliminary to official action, good or bad. Names humanise, are a part of the person. Numbers dehumanise. Brewer, 255771.)

Memory is the
well of life

NIGHT THOUGHTS

I

On Going to Bed.
'What dreams may come?'

Night thoughts are dream-thoughts
Fished up from God knows where, within
The teeming river of all human thought,
Where I and billions others float
In times and places where I've never been.
At night strange fragments swim by me,
Touching and sliding through my sleeping grasp,
Offering and withdrawing images   10
Beyond my art and heart, conditional
For visitation that no other may be made.
My sleeping thought is all men's memory,
A muddy river dimly known, in mists,
Where half-submerged I voyage till I sink,
Both as myself and others, in a company.

They visit me, or do I visit them,
Or am I them, 'never less in solitude
Than when I am alone'?

The fascination of this further world   20
Is clear but raises questions who I am
And where I go in puzzled waking thought.

II

11.30 p.m.
'And one is one and all alone
And ever more shall be so.'

Shall I be so alone? And never will
Unite with that grand whole,
That other One whose presence
Will absorb my absence, that unknown,
That sacrificial One who will demand   30
I lose myself to gain myself?
The darkness closes in; pinpoints
Of stars showing worlds past worlds
Of empty space that frightens me
With meaningless vacuity. Then nothing
Matters because matter's all.

III

Midnight.
'Tis now the very witching hour, when churchyards
yawn ... now could I drink hot blood.'

I make myself a cup of tea. The dead   40
Will only visit me in sleep. No sleep
Will come, and I have no revenge to take.

To have achieved great work
'That the world would not willingly let die'.
Or some great deed to mark
The passage of the years,
Would have been good. But neither I
Nor most of us have such a gift.
We run in some strange relay race
To carry a baton that we do not   50
Fully grasp, and sometimes drop;
Or take our turn 'in daily round and common task'
And lucky are we if so occupied, not scorned
Exiled, or beaten, or been starved to death
Or beaten, murdered, grieved or swindled others.

Some blink of light as from the speckled stars
Now shining through the kitchen window-pane,
Has given joy and some direction here
That daylight blinds me to. Go back to bed.

IV

1 a.m.   60
'Let us now praise famous men.'

At this small hour let us now praise great men,
Who never bothered with morals
Nor worried about others,
Were charming and ruthless,
Clever men, honoured by the state,
Men who wrote memoirs
And boasted of conquests,

Their successful cheating
And avoidance of duty,   70
Were interviewed in newspapers,
Chattered on television.
May they get their reward.
How I envy and despise them.
For some I have known, modest men,
Faithful servants of duty,
Only craven in fear of hurting,
Who did the dull jobs
Without complaining. Their
Reward is their virtue.   80
Their name is forgotten for evermore.
Their satisfaction is death.

V

2 a.m.
'Love is not love which alters when it
    alteration finds.'

The night is not still. The old house
Argues with itself about past presences,
Arthritic stairs groan. Outside the wind
Is up and crying. The trees toss in distress
And protest. The moon hurries through clouds.
The flickering stars shift though I cannot hear   90
The music of the spheres. Nothing is fixed
Even your face, dead-smooth, that yesterday
Was wrinkled in smiles of years survived
And soon will grin again in horror.

Nothing rests, is still, not even death,
But memory and darkness may recall.

The church, so long ago, was locked; At last
We found the keeper of the ancient key.
The door groaned open on the chilly vast
Of rounded arch where it was hard to see   100
What had been holy ground in times long past,
Or what was of more interest to me,
Yourself that on my dazzled eye still cast
Bright light; you only saw that dark must be.
Well was it that I could not hold you fast
So I can feed on loss eternally.

VI

2.30 a.m.
'I cried to sleep again.'

They swim to me through soft waters of sleep,
They rise to consciousness, the men I knew,   110
Now far away and not concerned with me.
The names of some are cut in stone or set
In books of youthful gallantry soon lost,
And others faded or now fade from life
With no memorial but in my thought
Of them; and when I die last echoes
Of their words and deeds will disappear.
We shared green spring, the yellow summer with
The sharp blue sky and walked in mud and snow.
And girls were faintly known, sharply desired,   120

The images of unknown paradisal joys.
Their laughter fades into the past, which now,
My memory recreates more rich and rare,
Mysterious still. And memory goes
Far back, into redeeming depths of time.
I walk in ancient places, suffer old
Injustices, or taste some lordly joys
With company, a wondering fulfilment
Or wonderfilled uncertainty, despair.
I hear the men come back to tell their tale   130
Of Emmaus, men wakened out of sleep.
Why them? I ask, and look
At their enlightened eyes, and see
They are the boys I walked with as a boy
When unbelief was like a wrestling game
And neither win or lose made difference.
The world was then, is now, more jangled
Than I thought.
My mind brings back what's gone yet is not gone.
What now? Who later will sustain the load   140
Of memory's inspiration? Will they care,
The ones who follow when we're dead?
The intellectual darkness covers all.
Let healing springs of dream pour over me.

VII

3 a.m.
'What should such fellows as I do, crawling
      between
Heaven and Earth?'

I dreamed I was a Jew. In a dark town
Two men – were they soldiers? – stopped me.
   I spoke
Italian. They were unimpressed. I ran,   150
Then in a boat I floated on a lake,
A mirror which reflected nothingness.
The engine stalled. No matter, I could
Use an oar as paddle. I was strong in arm.
Someone was after me, but I was looking for
Another. Coasting the shore I glimpsed
Through darkness soldiers bathing, laughing loud,
But they were Germans. Silent, I slid away.
What pursuit? What search? Of people, Age
   or Youth?
The lake was smooth but the boat so low   160
The water lipped the gunwale as to drink
The airy breath held in its hollowness.
I was the boat; would no one come to help?
The silvery moon looked down and did not care,
And laughter sounded from the farther shore.

VIII

4 a.m.
Nox perpetua.

If day will only come,
Sunshaft spear the night,
Fling the black rag behind,   170
Hurl my sweaty thought-blanket away,
Bring blood-warm light,

Call beyond the foolish
Premature cockcrow,
Send sparkling fresh streams
Over the arid pastures of thought.
But the black curtain hangs still,
The clock does not move.
The slow drip of dark
Fouls stagnant pools of thought.   180
Yet day must come, unless
This death-blanket crush me utterly,
But then Lord may I throw it off.

IX

5 a.m.
'Tis not in mortals to command success,
But we'll do more, Sempronius, we'll deserve it.'

Accept the failure of your dearest hopes
And taste the bitter drink for what it's worth,
As healing preparation for your death.
Throw off protective clothes. Accept   190
The naked self as what is truly there.
Reduce to singularity of aim
The multiple unreal ambitious wish.
Avoid comparisons with better men
And let all those who can, be satisfied.
Familiar words, though part forgot, will guide
The memory through mazed experience,
An old man stumbling in familiar ways.
The path leads on through houses, fields and woods

To known resorts, high peaks, dark groves of power,200
The sacred places where the memory lives,
Which being recognised are not the same.
The paths of memory are not clear; they bend
To new desires and may mislead the old,
Demanding back the strength they seemed to give,
And spiral downwards in a false return.
Yet there are landmarks still, and glades of joy,
Climactic hills of satisfied desire,
Beside the wasted lands of burnt-out wish,
Of ill-conceived misunderstood attempts,   210
Of questions left unasked, things better left
Unsaid, undone. The self revisiting
Though still the same, does not repeat the steps
Which once walked gladly, ignorantly, there,
But now knows, differently, not more,
Still seeking for the unknown mystery,
Which recollection of the good will not
Unfold but will give strength to find and lose
What must be lost with grace, rise with new life.

1991

ELUDED GRASP

High summer spread before me in the early day;
The river air brought scent of thyme and fresh-cut hay;
Running, I snatched the flowering meadow-sweet that sprung
Beside the path, but missed it; and a nettle stung.

SEEN FROM THE TRAIN

Battered old lady, Mother England,
Encrusted with decaying oldfashioned industrial jewels,
And too much clothed in shabby domesticity,
But still your breath smells sweet as hay,
Your skirts are green and leafy
And through torn clothing flashes a girl's wild thigh.

Mine eyes dazzle

FIAT LUX

I

IN THE BEGINNING

'Let us' said God, using the Trinitarian 'we',
'Set up the universe', and with the Very Word
Self-creating, created the other than himself,
From densely black anti-being, awaiting the spark.
'Let there be light' said God 'so we can see
What's cooking'. Explosively he fired the gas,
The galaxies hurtled out startled, sparkling,
Billions of bright fiery leaping lights
Springing joyfully across aeons of black space.
Then time began, dancing to a steady beat.   10
'But only we', thought God, 'can see this glory'.
Thinking sent the Word to describe the light.
'Let us now' said God, 'create more minds
To catch the light in telescopes of intellect,
To reflect'; so he started the tiny runners
Who led, gasping for breath, to the race of man.
Then their minds were so dazzled by the beauty
Of either sex, and sunshine and rain, and all
The splendour of mountains and plains,
The rivers, waterfalls, flowers, leaves, and fruit,   20
And the depths of the earth and the height
Of the stars, the sun and moon, the silvery fishes,

The swooping birds, horses and beasts that galloped,
Soft lambs and cruel tigers and serpents,
And most of all each other when young, and what
They could make, imitating God, their children,
Adornments, and houses and churches, then machines
And factories, and most of all self-contemplation
In poetry, music, art, and dance-halls, museums.
And greedy they became, contentious, murderous
    too, so   30
That they could not see God for the glory.
For the glory so bright dazzled their eyes,
And beneath the light always lay darkness profound
The original anti-being, seeking its own life,
That soon broke into part of that light. So God
Decided to enter that darkness, see
For himself, understanding the nature of things.
But the darkness comprehended him not,
For that was its nature, opposing the Sun,
Though now darkness depended on light to be known, 40
Had changed to become the blackness of lighted space.
God saw that with light you cannot avoid dark.

II

FIRST LIGHT

'Stand-to', hissed out in darkness down the line.
The silent pregnancy of night concludes
Though all is quiet yet, time not begun.
We stir limbs stiff with sleeping cold, to stare
At nothing, waiting for what we do not know;

What monster birth will crash upon our world?
Attack, or dull endurance? The bolts
Of rifles click and make us jump. We hold   50
Our breaths as in the faintest lightening from
The coming day dim shapes seem to emerge
– Or are they shades within our own eye-balls?
– 'But, Christ! they're coming!' 'No, they're not!'
Or will the barrage soften us to pulp?
Still silence. Darkness is almost grey.
The dawn wind shivers. Our devoted minds
Await the revelation of the fire,
Not warmth but frenzied surging bringing death.
'I wish to Christ I could get out of here.'   60
Yes, we will go. The light is here. We have
Survived the night, the dawn. Now face the day.

III

ELY CATHEDRAL.
PASCAL SERVICE
MIDNIGHT 1975

Muffled in iron cold, in darkness like
The primal emptiness, we stand, silent,
The walls invisible, no stars, no sky
Awaiting the first prick of flame.

The spark leaps up, and space is given. We have
Our faces now, and limits. Let the staff
Plunge, let the font respond with burning life,   70
And gain and lose, renew, die to revive.

The shadows dance within the expectant nave.
They owe their life to light's uncertain life.

We shuffle in a crowd towards the east,
Led by a wavering electric torch
Uncertainly to hear the happy fault
Faultlessly intoned that brought us foolish here,
The dull grey middle-aged ordinary folk,
None at all noble, few intelligent,
The sweaty men in shabby overcoats,   80
The yawning children bored and looking round,
Smooth curates reeking still of after-shave,
Old ladies delicately scented with mothballs,
Creation's latest, evolution's best,
All come to see the light, leaving for the dark,
Potential tinder for the living spark.

IV

BOSTON MUSEUM OF FINE ARTS

First, the American forefathers, high-lighted
In black, not mourning but unsmiling, alive
To destiny, Bible on knee, their children
Formed in their image, sober creators   90

Themselves, in their generations, of wealth
That brought the brown shine of mahogany
From the Old World, brighter silver, then Impressionists
Of light, and at last can present their own,

The latest thing, a corridor of mirrors,
New World; pure mechanics, costly and precise,
Reflecting us infinitely, mindlessly,
Ourselves our own art subjects, brilliantly meaningless.

Reality repeats, defeats, itself in glass.
Sharp illusion cuts the boundaries of sense.   100
Our unpersoned images mock us endlessly,
Both outer world and inward sight destroyed.

We are come by this bright mirror-box
Into the world of light, a modern heaven.
No darkness shadowed here, no mystery,
Save endless repetition without sense.

Behind the images no depth, no life,
No mind, no cause, only our surfaces
Forever. Someone anonymous,
A calculator, fabricated glass.   110

Was dying Gauguin troubled in foresight of this,
This visibility, in that last gloomy great
Picture of spoilt Eden, the trees dark snakes of indigo,
Dim vistas here, the grotesque idol pointing to Beyond?

What livid man is that, plucking the fruit?
Where is his Eve? Dusk darkens dawn. Where
    first Spring?
What parodic Graces are these naked brooding women?
What flowers are at their feet? Who that old man?

Where can they go, stricken into stillness?
What thoughts hold them or are held? Where are
    the gods,   120
Where Flora and her country mirth?
Tahiti pauses between old and new, old life, new death.

Outside, daylight retreats in cold clear skies.
The western clouds burn briefly with delight,
But I confuse the moon with lamps like her,
She rises slowly eastwards, earthbound too.

But soon she queens it over street and rail
Rejects our modern knowledge of her barren mass
Her light reflected, motion meaningless, renews
Her sacredness, high in the cold dark sky.   130

No art, metallic sheen, or self-sick thought
Restores us here, no knowledge of a truth
That certifies us in the world or out,
But natural brightness in the fated dark.

We need the dark to go to, our long home.
Let there be night to give us quiet rest.
But may the bright sun whose absence makes the dark,
And his reflective moon, visit our sleep.

For 'stand to' see above, p.41.

The section on Ely Cathedral is so precisely dated because it was in that year that the ancient Pascal service was performed, at first in absolute darkness at the West end, then after the fire lit in the font, the plunging staff, we moved into the light under the Octagon and the ninth century plain-song chant referring to Adam's 'happy fault' (because it led to Christ's redemptive incarnation) was superbly sung. Nowadays an emasculated form of the service takes place, with no fire, no staff, no chant, and concluding with communion and hymns.

In the section 'Boston Museum of Fine Arts', after the mention of the American 'primitive' portraits and the collections of fine furniture, eighteenth and nineteenth century silver, and Impressionist paintings which the sitters amassed, the reference is to a temporary exhibition of modern art in October 1989 when the main exhibit was a corridor of mirrors some thirty feet long, six feet high, three feet wide, in which even the floor and ceiling were mirrors, as well as the internal and external walls. I have regrettably but perhaps significantly forgotten the name of the artist/engineer. The work contrasted with Gauguin's 'last great gloomy painting'. What? Whence? Whither? *painted in the consciousness of his rapidly approaching death, and now itself too frail to be moved from the MFA.*

The Gauguin painting may well be taken as a kind of melancholy, serious parody of Botticelli's Prima Vera, *even if it were not intentionally so. It seems to be a testimony both to disillusionment with the earthly paradise that Tahiti had first appeared to be, and to a foreboding of deeper disillusionment, or loss of meaning, to come. The Keatsian parodic allusions are obvious enough. For Section II line 16 compare I Corinthians 26, 'not many wise men after the flesh, not many mighty, not many noble, are called'.*

1990

Take heart of grace

MORS IANUA VITAE

GREAT UNCLE ALEC

Great Uncle Alec was a simple man,
Small, with a limp and a stiff arm, due to
A mix-up with an ill-thrown grenade
At sweet seventeen. That ill-throw blew some good
With high explosive and flung him into
Hospital in nineteen seventeen, when so few
Of his mates came back. But he came back,
Though not until, before they fitted him together,
He saw the pearly gates and heard the angels sing.
He thought it all a bit too posh for him,   10
The poor boy from the bottom of the class.
It was a different style of life from what he'd known.
He came back from ethereal bliss to see his mates
(Who must have gone before him had he known),
So turned to London's dark familiar streets,
And modestly with his stiff arm he earned
A meagre wage French-polishing brown tables,
Creating brightness more familiar,
Less dazzling than that heavenly glimpse, though less
Reflective. It showed a better job,   20
Despite his limp, a postman's, so he trudged
The unreflecting grimy streets, come rain or shine,
To pass on messages that he would never learn,
And never to him, but faithfully delivered.

An unknown stream of knowledge flowed through him.
A limping wingless unquicksilver Mercury
In blue serge, unsullied by the lies he carried,
Unbrightened by the truths in his brown bag.
He then must push at many different gates,
And learnt that opening gates revealed new life,   30
But not for him. Who knows what one may find?
A limping man, he saw strange sights but met
No father to adore or kill. Some dogs might bark
    or bite,
But no three-headed Cerberus, no damsel merciless
Or merciful confronted him. He never saw
Again in pain the brilliant pearly gates,
To his relief, but found the great house doors
Were always shut, save for the narrow slit,
More narrow than a needle's eye, to grasp
His missive and resist himself, his errand done.   40

A decent life, a useful honest brave
And friendly one – does it lack poetry?
It asks some questions; he did not. Nor
In his eighties was he at all keen
To approach those mighty doors of gleaming pearl,
Enter that fuller life he once had glimpsed,
Where perhaps his mates, reconstituted
After being blown to bits, sat on soft clouds,
And in their crowns sang by the glassy sea.
Perhaps he thought the inner doors were shut,   50
A fuller life was more than he could take;
Or probably, like most, he did not think.

AN OLD FASHIONED BURIAL

The graveyards usually strike their chill. The aged
Bring their own winter-death. Sometimes the earth
Is too frozen for the grave-digger as if
Reluctant to accept more human dross.
Denies its motherhood. The old have no place
On or in the earth. But earth relents,
Or is forced; another rape by pick and shovel,
A forced fertility sprouts graveyard stone.   60
But underneath, the earth is mother-warm,
Covers the dissolution in a healing dark.
Oblivion spreads from it like a scent
As turf enfolds and flowers and visits cease.
But this day it was hot, the diggers sweated,
And sweat answered for their tears, while for some
Who stood by paralysed with grief
The tears answered for sweat, for this little box
Held a spring death. The grave opened easily,
And our hope entered in it too easily for   70
Our despair. Our loss was conventional.
We had hardly come to know him. We had
Seen him so briefly, he had just come to laugh.
He had known the fearful panic of the endless dark,
But knew that crying brought comfort and joy,
As we now know it never can again.
He knew the joy of hunger satisfied,
While we shall starve for ever in our hearts.
He knew the opening door that brought delight
And then he slipped upon the frightening slope   80
And missed our grasp, to find what other door?

He could not even crawl. No bodiless cherub,
His needs were imperious. Who satisfies them now?
But now he has no needs. His need is ours.
The grave is filled and our hearts empty.
Untrained in worldly ways (no worse for that)
He leaves us too well schooled in pain,
But not so well learned that we kept him from
Those dread mysteries of God, the gates of death;
What hope we had of him remains our life.   90

THE PREACHER

That is no gate to beat upon, beat down,
The key a stab of pain or sharp syringe,
And opening with slow grinding hinge, to let
Us peer beyond into the unknowable;
No darkness even, as no consciousness,
No time, no light, beginning nor an end,
Except the end of struggle, horror, joy.
Is that not so? Can we imagine else?
Have others all gone to a world of light,
To leave us hopeful, self-deceiving here?   100
We always look for mirrors that give back
Inordinate variety which we
In ignorance believe is life. Not so.
There must be difference from what we think,
Imagine, hope or fear. From positive
Comes negative, and so we lose all sense.
If we are shut within this living box
And nothing lies outside the box, the box
Itself is solipsistic fantasy.

No exit, then no entrance or inside,   110
No purpose or significance in life.
We know that is not so. To find the door
Is no hard search: it lies all round,
The walls fall down, the gates are open wide,
Though what they show we are too blind to see.

THE FARMER

Each day's enough for me, its good and bad;
Let clever men speak long words as they will.
The gate of death, five-barred, soon opens out,
The catch an old and simple one. I see
Through it the sunny pastures, not too dry,   120
With hedges, woods, and on the hill a tower,
Like our church tower, four square and battlemented,
With elms (immortal, I suppose) such as I used to see,
Which cluster round a walled grave-yard.
Then I will walk those fields with their spring flowers,
As they used to be in England, till I come
To the grave-yard, with the old brown stones
A bit askew, and even the marble chippings
Of recent graves lit in a softening light,
And a convenient hole left there for me,   130
All warm and welcoming, seed-bed like,
And company. So I'll slip down there,
Beside my Lily, as if in our old double bed,
And she will touch my side and lie quite close.
(She always spread herself) and so I'll say
'Shove over a bit my dear', as once I did,
And no grandchild will wake us with night fears.

We'll comfortably sleep, and then wake up;
The trumpets will sound and we shall be free
For who knows what an interesting day?   140

FELL WALKER

I climb more slowly and my breath is short.
The day darkens, clouds lower, mist smokes up.
The path is rougher and the wind is cold.
The flowery meadows now are patchy turf,
The rocks make stumbling work. My friends
Are left behind or gone ahead. The map
Is vague, the path less clear, no birds now sing.
Yet driven on, I reach the uncertain crest,
I thrust, or am thrust, as I choke, beyond,
I plunge in darkness, giddy with the fall.   150
But see, I float sensationless in fields
Of air. New light pierces me, a radiance
Surrounds, freedom from effort and desire,
No lack but lightness given and joy
Accompany me all the days of my death.

WE ARE ALL PRISONERS OF OURSELVES

Furnish the bleak cell
Bribe the gaoler to
Pack it with what others sell
For comfort, beauty, joy.

What do I use for a bribe?   160
My hopes, loves, virtue, fear.

Give them against the jibe
That nothing has value here.

Then dissatisfied still
We ask for company.
One comes with a will.
Love her or die.

Then we fill up the cell,
We need more room.
And who can tell   170
If release will come?

Sometimes the gaoler
Tells us of other places,
Of our own failure
To show the right faces.

What was the sentence?
Who was the judge?
When will we go hence?
What gate can we budge?

There is nothing to do   180
But love one another:
Whatever we rue
The darkness will cover.

'You have done well'
The gaoler may say

'In your little cell,
But why did you stay?

The door was not shut,
Though you clung all together,
In this miserable hut   190
Away from fine weather.

I have fed you for long
Now your time's at an end;
Now seek to be strong
Whether you stand up or bend.

Go out from the dark,
Take courage in hand;
As if from the ark
Walk on heavenly land.

The doors will not hold,   200
Go into the sun;
Faint-heart, be bold,
Your suffering is done.

Great Uncle Alex is taken from the life.

A limping man. Oedipus is sometimes thought to have limped.

Cerberus. The three-headed dog in Greek myth that guarded the entrance to Hades. A watchdog.

Damsel merciless. La Belle Dame sans Merci; fatal attraction.

Mother-warm. Freshly-dug graves are relatively warm, being out of the wind.

World of light. Henry Vaughan.

* 1992

SURVIVAL

In the concentration camp, said the old man,
We lived together
In the dead cold
By making a human oven. Piled up in a
Heap of humanity those inside
Were warm but could not breathe.
Insides out! Stunned by the cold,
Turned inside, some, crushed by weight of love,
Fought out again to breathe.
But breath without warmth
Congeals in icy patterns.
Each could give life to others
With warmth that would not keep himself alive.
Could save each other with warmth
By exchange
That could not keep each single one alive.
We die alone.

This is based on episodes remembered by a survivor of the concentration camps.

RIDDLES UNWISELY EXPOUNDED

I

A fish without water,
Summer without green growth,
Lightning without rain;
– Struggle, heat, dry light.

II

A mill without corn
A lonely tower
A broken arch,
A bolt that does not clinch,
A wind seeking a sail.

III

A line of clothes without a prop.

IV

A punchball
On a slackening spring;
Kicked upstairs
Should be kicked downstairs.
Impatient tyrant,
Bends to every rumour;
Transparently devious
Never making himself clear;

A simple-minded man
Though super-subtle schemer;
Father-figure to a lot of bastards;
Nature's busybody,
Idle as they come.
Why doesn't he go?
But who would have him?

V

Has a dragging coat
A running sore
A hole in his pocket
A weight on his back
And a buzzing in his ears,
But will speak with confidence
To the enemies in the gate.

VI

Has a crutch, a cushion,
A goad, and ointment,
A stone in his shoe,
And an uneasy conscience.

VII

The veteran of a thousand skirmishes,
Defensive, but sends out fighting patrols,
Conceals the scars of the biting word,
The snide comment, respectful insult;

He rides out the bluster, as wild and wet
As the southwest storm. Occasional victor
Undeserving and unrecognised; master
Of some well-planned defeats and his own
Exasperation before dumb insolence.
Forgetful, corrected, hopeful, a batsman
Who stays though so often bowled out.
He moves his grey head side to side, looks around,
Like a baited bull, modern Sebastian
The target of so many sharp arrows,
Must watch for the next move, not speak too much,
Nor ever complain, but seizing the moment to strike
He moves his head side to side like a snake.

I   *A man without children*

II   *A man without a woman*

III   *A woman without a man*

IV   *The Master of a College (or a Prime Minister, or head
of a company)*

V   *A father (cf. Psalm 127, 5)*

VI   *A husband*

VII   *The chairman*

All men are brothers

LLASA

The Pope established an Apostolic Vicariat of Mongolia in 1844 and two members of the French Lazarist Order (a congregation of secular priests living under religious vows with specific responsibility for missions), MM. Huc and Gabet, were selected to gather information and preach the Word. At first established in Peking, where they were treated with hostility and acquired a lasting dislike for Chinese materialism and tyranny, they then undertook a remarkable journey to Lhasa, enduring extreme hardships, through countries hardly then known to the West. On arrival at Lhasa they were beginning to be so successful that the Chinese Ambassador Ki-Chan forced them to return to China and eventually to Europe. The Abbé Huc published a substantial two volume account in Paris about 1848 of their three-year journey, 1844-46. This was translated by W. Hazlitt in the early 1850s (third edition, London, 1856), as Travels in Tartary, Thibet and China.*

Huc writes with fullness and wit. Gabet's part seems to have been mainly a supportive silent and stoic endurance of suffering. Huc after his return to France eventually relinquished his orders, though not his faith, married and had a family.

The poem attempts, using a few episodes from the book, to distil something of the efforts, expectations and desires that impelled the missionaries to Lhasa, with some commentary.

The Abbé Huc speaks
In the beginning
    To serve the altar through the coloured year,
    Small boy by gaunt priest
    In France's fertile fields
    Was then my spirit's feast.

    When older my soul fattened on thin wafers
    Impressed with the triumph of pain.
    I chose an election
    But found too flat the plain.

    I sought heights, strangeness, ignorance,   10
    Swallowed hard at strange food
    I burnt to melt frozen hearts
    The hardest way was my only good.

The journey
    Then hot Chinese hatred turned me so
    That love drove me into the cold
    With strange companions,
    The camel born to servitude,
    The white horse obedient to the rein,
    The little black mule, used to burdens,   20
    Silent friend Gabet, ready to suffer,
    Ugly Samdadchiemba, awkward convert,
    To redeem the lost millions,
    The shivering souls in the waste deserts.

    We did not seek enlightenment: we went
    To bring the light, the light of the world,

To those who lived in darkness but might seem,
I thought, a little like what Providence
Divine had made of me who have the honour
Unworthy though I be, of being French, 30
And Catholic, and Christian, a priest.
They were not quite bereft of spirit, for God
Has made the lama as a shadow of the priest
His mind receptive, as I thought, a cup
Which I might fill with holy blood of life.

So Providence Divine by means so strange
As Chinese hate of anything but gain,
Then gave me hope of conquering the vast
And barren wastes, the mountains and the cold
Where God had left his people desolate, 40
A hungry flock that called out to be fed
By us with transubstantial wine and bread.

Missionaries

We lamas of the Western Sky took yellow robes
Red sash and jacket, yellow cap,
A purple velvet collar, shaved our heads,
(Strange transformations of black robes, soutane,)
To make ourselves less strange, unchanged within.
We thought to challenge then some evil ways:

We joined the pilgrimage to see the Bokte 50
Carve up himself, the spirit conquering flesh.
He would take up the sacred knife from off
His knees, plunge it within, spurt red,
Then prophesy, scream, drink his blood.

Perversion of self-sacrifice, yet holy
In perversion; the devil has his miracles.
We would prevent, pray the great prayer,
Pray God to shame the devil, let the Bokte die.

By miracle we'd stop the miracle,
Let the crowd tear us, or bow down to love   60
A greater spirit than ours or his.
Grand anticlimax. We lost our way.
The sand hills shifted and we wandered wide.
And holy chance pulled down our pride.

On the way
A hard coming we had of it indeed,
We brought the light, not sought the star,
For that world knew it not. Why did God
Create a wilderness like Ortous?
Yet there is beauty: We passed a narrow opening   70
Between two rocks, their summits lost in clouds.
Then as it were, within a garden enclosed
– Oh Mary! – lay a spring where waters flowed
Between the banks lined with angelica
And sweet-scented mint. There we camped
And lit our fire and cooked our venison.
Then like a thunderbolt an eagle dropped
And, with great claws snatched up, and
      mighty wings,
So carried off our meat. In paradise
We learnt that nature will bring sacrifice.   80

The Unredeemed
The pagans live in eternity, the boundless sky
Enfolds them, clear or fog. Mountain or plain
Endlessly extend, no difference, all centre
Circumference limitless, never reached; no past
No future beyond the circling day and night,
And change that is no change. The gods are ever
Present, to be propitiated
Because disaster daily comes, and fear
Eternal drives men on, but hope is born   90
Like children every day to die away
But endlessly to reappear and cry,
Sometimes to laugh and live, but to no point.
The aim of life is to prevail. Anger helps,
Fierce quarrels, conquest and above all
The unremitting toil for grain and herd.
We bring to them the history, mystery, of love,
To learn what's past is past, the future new,
Bring gospel hope, bring heaven into view.

The hard high road   100
The world is bleached of colour, only snow
That blinds us with the brightness of the world
Makes us look inward for our need to know.

From off the precipice a mule is hurled
By burdened icy slip to rocky death.
We stagger on the path, stiff bundles furled

In shapeless cloth, and like a knife our breath
Cuts through our straining lungs: through threads
    we peer
With painful sight to keep the narrow faith

To which we cling above the abyss of fear   110
Of nothingness that mindlessly has curled
Snakelike to swallow down all meaning here.

The frozen man
    The cold clutched at us with an icy hand.
    For all our clothes our very hearts were chilled.
    The horses dropped and died. Still up we climbed.
    The camels splayed four-footed wide on ice.
    We found a traveller sitting on a stone,
    His head bent forward on his chest, his arms
    Held tight around his sides, himself unmoved.   120
    We called. He did not speak. 'O foolish man
    To linger so, to let the blood then freeze'.
    We recognized the human block, a lama,
    Young man, who used to call upon us in
    Our tent to hear us speak the Sacred Word.
    His face like wax, his eyes like glass, half closed,
    And from his nostrils and his mouth there hung
    Bizarrely, icicles. His friends had left him.
    We took him up and wrapped him warm.
    But he soon died. And many men, like him   130
    Were left, not dead, to die with frozen hearts,
    Except God's scavengers, the vultures then,
    Impatient, pecked at eyes, tore living flesh,
    Until we hoped for rapid death to free

Their souls, to go to where ignorance and pain
Would earn from the almerciable God
Eternity of rest and praise. Yet that
One man we tried to save will haunt me still
Until I die: paralysis of will,
The immobility of frozen flesh,   140
The essence of humanity a block,
The heart unable to be opened to
The truths we showed through images of pain
Of God himself; unspeaking misery
So deep that it became the man himself.
And yet our spirit moved us on, we came
To Lhasa, Land of Spirits, where the rocks
Themselves, the barren landscape, spoke in terms
Of worship of strange gods who know no pain.
Where words carved on the rocks gave calm advice,   150
And fear was only due to nature and to man;
The Word seen not as flesh; unfeeling stone
Sufficient to the day itself alone.

Lhasa, unforbidden city
We came to Lhasa after eighteen months,
Surmounted the last mountain, worst of all
We had encountered, but all Mongols all
Tibetans knew it as remission for
All sins – and penance was it even for us
Though whether for all sins we might well doubt.   160
From long before the dawn, nine hours we toiled
To reach the top, then at the setting sun
We reached the plain and saw the noble city.
The centre of the Buddhic world. A wall

Of ancient trees encircles it, green-girdling
The tall white houses, with red or yellow doors,
With dirty stinking muddled rooms inside,
An easy parable of their spiritual life.
The curling gilded roofs of many temples
And palaces surround the holy mount.   170
And as a sign of God, gold roofed, shines high
The temple of the Dalai Lama, wrapped
In silence absolute as of the sky
Without a cloud, in holy meditation;
But down on earth deep fear of the Chinese;
Their edicts end with 'Tremble and obey'.
We thought that God would help resist their power
And this is no forbidden city except
To Englishmen, invaders from the West.
What natural religion had set up   180
We thought our supernatural would crown.

To succeed is to fail
     At first the chapel of us French priest-lamas
     Was source of interest and we spread
     The evangelical seed on ground
     That promised to be fertile. Mysticism
     And piety grow strong in that thin air,
     Where body turns to spirit as wax to flame.
     Lhasa is the abode of men of prayer,
     Except for the Chinese. And soon Ki-Chan   190
     The Emperor's ambassador, as one
     Who feared to see our seedlings grow, and men
     Find independence in our loving God,
     Expelled us for our virtue and success.

He claimed he would protect the Dalai Lama's
Faith – a foul hypocrisy we could not fight.
We did not wish to give excuse for him
To conquer all Tibet with Chinese power,
The Devil seeking what he might devour.

Only failure can succeed   200
O where shall justice and mercy be found?
Who shall protect for men the spirit of peace?
Lamas are killed, temples cast to ground.

The inner-directed silence will cease
The screams of the wounded mount up to the sky
Only by death can they find release.

The power and the joy can only defy,
By losing the battle, material force.
The spirit to live, must learn how to die.

As strength fails and virtue dries up at source   210
Courage shall be keener and never comply,
Accept nothing evil, refuse to endorse,

And never surrender, never mind why,
But follow our Master wherever the course,
And down in his company loyally lie.

Epilogue

What really drove us on? I do not deny
Sincere conviction in our conscious minds,
The strength of our desire to spread the Word;
But was it not some deeper need – the wish   220
To know, to find, as well as bring a newer truth?
We failed; we brought on only trouble to
Tibet and to ourselves. Our sufferings were
Adventurous satisfaction, but we failed.
The whole long freezing effort was a waste,
A cold wind blowing dead and useless dust.
As old age comes I think of our conceit,
Our lack of questioning ourselves, our truth.
I see grandchildren playing round my house,
And easy deference now tolerates   230
Deficiencies of age that poisons all.
My travels earn polite respect. And yet
I failed in all but travelling so far
For purposes that hardly knew themselves.
They were not false, but strange and strangeness was
The pull of Lhasa's city of spiritual power,
Tranquillity within the sordidness.
And so it was my ignorance that drew
Me searching forward, though assuming that
I brought what I was really looking for.   240
I failed with ignominy but failure is
The essence of my calling. To be called
Is, and had I known it, was the most
That I could hope for. Lhasa called me; then
Sent me away. I came, I saw, I failed.
But now I think that failure is the truth.

Perhaps that was my Master's message then
As now, chilled by old age, I sit by fires
And dream of hidden Paradise high up,
Where children play their useless noisy games   250
And purposes are self-fulfilling there.

1996

WATERLOO

We ordinary men who try to do our best,
Which is only ordinary (some less than that)
May wonder at the extraordinariness of one
Great man, who if he had not escaped
From Elba would not have caused the death
On that one ordinary day and field
Of fifty thousand mostly ordinary men
Whose bright uniforms he coloured with blood,
Transformed them in various ways but
In no way for their good. And now he is
Adored in the Visitors' Centre and Museum
Where Wellington and Blücher are hardly seen,
And Frenchmen think of Waterloo as victory,
Which shows how extraordinary he was
And reveals his secret, that he gave ordinary men
The chance we crave to be other, to escape
Our ordinary selves, as so many did that day
Into glory. How the Imperial Guard advanced
In blue and white tunics, bravado of shako,
In regular step, rank upon rank,
Comrades in arms, splendour of France,
Remorselessly up the slope, rat-a-tat-tat,
The drummer-boys beating to keep the step,
Invincible army, proudly with banners,
Exaltation and grimness, triumph at hand.
The thin English lines lay hid in await.
Then the redcoats stood up from the rye and
At fifty yards distance poured thousands and
Thousands of bullets to tear away flesh,

And the front ranks crumpled then all the rest
And bravery met its extraordinary end,
And Wellington waved high his hat and all
The Allies charged down and the battle was won,
And the extraordinary triumphed over both sides
Because one man wanted it more than life,
And persuaded so many they were not so ordinary.

Yet ordinariness survives, though death may strike
On Waterloo's fields and seasonal crops,
Ground folded like ruckled eiderdowns
Of mud and green, hard bed for so many,
Where in an afternoon fifty thousand men
Who had not slept or eaten for a night and a day,
Were soaked by June rain of the most ordinary kind,
Among ordinary crops, having screamed and shot
Each other, enriched the ordinary soil
With their blood and the looters with their
Ordinary watches, boots, jewels and purses:
They disappeared and soon ordinary ground
Had gulped them into ordinary pits no more
To be seen. The ground stayed. Napoleon fled
And Wellington wept. A victory is great tragedy
Only defeat a greater, and tragedy
Is said to ennoble, redeems our day
But ordinariness is more pleasing, has
More sense if less excitement. When all's said
Though death is extraordinary we like
To postpone it, to cherish the ordinary,
Till death, as on that day, itself becomes
Ordinary.

POET TO PROPHET

(After Dante, Paradiso, *xiii, 130-141)*

Don't be so sure of what you can foresee,
And think the root will always give the flower;
The chickens and the eggs may not agree;

For I have seen beneath the winter shower
The thorn stand rigid, sharp and coarse,
That later bore the rose in its due hour:

And I have seen a ship that ran with force
Swift and direct, at last upon the sill
Of home trip up and perish in its course.

So when you've seen one picking at the till,
Another make a gift, you must not think
That you see with the eye of God, for still
The one may rise up high, the other sink.

Chè rado sotto benda
Parola oscura giunge allo 'ntelletto
Dante, *Canzone* X, 57–8

NICODEMUS

NICODEMUS, A VERY OLD MAN,
MEDITATES ON HIS LIFE

Nicodemus is said to have been an historical figure. The Encyclopaedia
Biblia, *ed. Cheyne and Black, 1903, s.v. seems tentatively to identify him
with Nicodemon, son of Gorion, one of the three or four richest and most
important men in Jerusalem, and I have accepted this. His special duty
was to provide water for the pilgrims that came up for feasts, elaborated
and referred to here, 11. 14–5, and elsewhere. I have not used the EB's
further speculations, and have rejected the ancient tradition that he
became a Christian. Since he was a Pharisee and a 'ruler in Israel' I have
taken him to be a lawyer and a learned man, a conscientious and efficient
administrator, and have attributed to him the editing of a minor text, as
well as an ambivalent, if not inconsistent character.*

*Whatever the historical basis, it is clear that he is also an 'exemplary'
figure in the Gospel according to John, illustrating among other things
those problems of the relations between words and things, and of the nature
of metaphorical (or prophetic, poetic, fictional) language in its relation to
'truth', which are continuing concerns of the Gospel as a whole. The poem
is designed as a series of meditations on such problems, as they may be
focussed in the figure of Nicodemus.*

I

I fulfilled the Law many years
After. Sat on committees, made righteous judgments
Of true and false; paid taxes justly,
Was not too greedy, stifled my lusts,
Contested foolish idealism and ill-will,
And, even worse, the tedium of contesting
Folly and ill-will; attempted to purify
The muddy torrent of fashionable cant,
Slogans, clichés, ridiculous metaphors,
For the sake of Justice and Law,   10
For Humanity, therefore. No one heard
How I had helped or betrayed
Or had failed, if I had. I continued my work.

II

The waters of purification
Flowed, thanks to my organisation,
As still they flow, bringing me honour
And wealth; to all, cleanness
To make life worth living, living worth life.
One does not live by bread alone,
Nor by spirit, but by keeping things going.   20
I had a vision, now a dream,
Of a good life for men on earth,
Peace and good will; full stomachs,
The robe white, the swept and garnished room
Holding the scoured dish, the golden
Orange for the contented child,

Secured by sanitation and protective police.
Do you mock these ordinary, unpoetic,
These necessary things?
Dirt and disorder defile us today;   30
'The earth lies polluted under its inhabitants,
For they have transgressed the Laws, violated
      the statutes.'
Our cities are dark, dusty and dangerous,
Deserts are scattered with cameldung and cactus,
Dry bones and shadowed valleys,
Where he is lost, whom I helped and betrayed.
Water is wanted for cleaning and growing,
An end to sin, a beginning of justice,
Fulfilment of the Law. Where, O where
Shall justice be found, the clean city?   40
These are the stalk and the petals,
The green tree, the living red of the yet unfound
Rose of the desert.

A foundation of rock, tender grass,
Sheep feeding near the paved city,
O Lord, by these things men live;
Not by words and metaphors,
Dry thoughts in hot heads,
But by Things, fed by living waters
That spring from rocks we must cleave,   50
To make green the grass, the grape oozy,
Sluice the streets, sweeten the sweaty,
Wash away thirst, purify
Desires to extinction.
Then justice will be established without hunger,

The Law fill the land to the coasts.
The deserts and the cities will sing a new song,
The trees on the hill-sides shall clap their hands
    with joy.
The embracing sea shall roar, and all that is in it.
The whirlwind over the waves, the clouds on the
    mountain-tops,   60
The fish in the rivers, the flowing cisterns never dry,
All marshalled to dance in orderliness,
Feeding ten times five thousands in social justice.
No man shall overcome another. The bruised reed
Shall be propped up, the dimly burning wick
    not quenched,
No man judged before he is heard:
Trees shall be planted, the wild waters channelled:
The purity of our lives, the goodness of God,
Shown in our own good works.

III

That was my vision, now my dream,   70
Fading now as I wake from life to death.
The stream of my life flowed calm and full
To cleanse, to make blossom the desert.
But the desert is too dry, my stream too thin,
Too shallow; it meanders and fails;
My life, like his, a failure, though of different kind.
My aim was regulated, worthy, not wasteful.
He offered himself as a drink
To those whose own hearts should have poured out
Rivers of living waters. Fine words.   80

But I made wet water really flow.
And, I thank God, I have always behaved very well
                    – Except perhaps once –
Paid tithes, fasted, given to charitable organisations,
Borne the boredom of my life's dutiful smooth waters
Without complaint, suppressed the knowledge
Of pain, those jagged rocks on which I flowed.

His life, how different. A rushing torrent
Leaping the rocks with rainbow spray,
Joyful, extravagant, wasteful, played in by children.,   90
Unowned, unchannelled, unfenced from filth,
Promiscuously drunk from, splashed with, washed in,
Plunging towards the waterfall
Of a thunderous chosen vertiginous death.
Such a force, so wasted.

We had this in common, beyond our humanity:
Each of us loved the Law. It was part of his mind,
More than memory. The carpenter's son needed
    no chisel
Of pen to scroll. He was no Scribe, but shaped by
    his father.
And here his weakness; the letter he did not love,   100
Though Teacher was neither lawyer nor scholar.
The fine scrolls in order round the room,
The earnest desk, he did not want. Wonderfully
Did he teach in the Synagogue. He never forgot a word,
Yet broke tradition, changed the words handed down.
The word was not sacred to him. He might have
    created it.

The literal sense was never his limit.
He could never have edited a text
As I, in my little spare time, have done.

Yet I, more than my colleagues, admired   110
His teaching. For a moment the burden was lifted.
I wanted to laugh and leap.
Why should I travel, so heavy-laden,
Carrying the dead past, struggling to master
The laws of the present, direct the ways to come?
Why seek honour at feasts, the best seat
At the Synagogue, to maintain law and order,
Against the very desires of men?
Why not be happy myself?

Absurd! The selfish man's plea   120
To be irresponsible. Can the desert blossom
Without canals? Can they be cut
Without making lazy men dig?
Can Love live without Law to guard her?
Does not sin defile and destroy?
The ways of the past are well-trodden through
    green pastures,
But the ways of the future wander through valleys
    of wilderness.
We must guard ourselves, no cloud-pillar will guide;
And no prophet will rise up from Galilee,
Say my colleagues, for whom, as for me,   130
Happiness is not the most important thing.

How I attacked them! They could not love him.
For myself, I attended to evidence, things, not words;
How he had driven traders from the Temple,
Changed water to wine
That makes glad the hearts of men digging
In fields and ditches.
He and I valued the same things
Though in a different order,
I being more logical looking at love   140
As crown, not fundament. But he
Called me, as I felt; which was why
In solitary night, down dirty lanes
I went seeking the son of light
And found a deep and dazzling darkness:
And turned back to the dimness of bright day.
I could not see by that dark sun.
I asked for bread, he gave me breath,
Words, not things; a highly metaphorical stone.

The torch flickered as if wings rushed by.   150
On dark and slippery paths I struggled up
To the more respectable parts. Sky withdrew
Its forces; the city recovered from night,
Rallied to bells, carts' crash, boys' shout.
Eye-beams not failing in darkness's infinity
Imprinted now with colour and shape
Stored the mind with the freshness of things.
Busy men sober and gray took care;
Friend nodded to friend; lovers parted
Promising soon to meet; the problem   160

At hand, the moment's compulsion, is all
We know, or need, or are likely to know.

But now I know that in each other
We meet ourselves; my rejection of him
Rejected myself, but my failure his,
And to fail is to betray both ourselves and others.
We are less alone than we think. My failure
Is also the end of a civilisation,
Of a people, their land, independence.
Israel is perishing, and the sand   170
On which I built the house of my endeavours
Slips away not in storm or war
But in absolute lack of sense and coherence.

When later the Council sent men to arrest him
Unavailing I spoke for due process of Law:
No man shall be judged unheard.
What more as a just man could I say?
When next I saw him he was dead.
I brought spices to embalm him,
As I wrap my texts in notes, defending my hurt mind, 180
To keep my mind sweet against the corrupting world,
For I felt he was my mind; but he was dead.

IV

What can I do with this mind of my death?
What contradiction this corruption
Collapse anarchy of atoms ruin
Of what I love my body my books
And decent institutions,
Choking the clean streets with offal?
Death infects the living. I hate death.

If I could choose an everlasting life,   190
To walk the high green hills of Galilee
Would be my wish, to watch the swelling slopes
That change with every step, the limestone springs
That wander through the leaf-pale copses bright
That bronze in autumn; hear the birds, and talk
With wife, friends, children through long years
    that held
No painful promise of deserting strength,
No anxious envy of competing men,
But brim full and more full of contemplative
Love and knowledge, knowing God as Love.   200
Loving to know God and men and all things
Blooming new and new and more and more
Till mind filled up black night with stars
That brightly needed dark and nothingness,
Creation's plus and minus reconciled
For evermore as day and night:
Heaven one long private sabbath calm,
Bettering the best of what I wish to be,
Disregarding failure, loss and change.   210

Yet this I cannot hope. What remains but failing?
My crazy body smells already sour.
The drifting acrid smokes and ghosts
Of Sheol and Gehenna swirl in my mind,
The rubbish-stinks of smouldering fire-fear.
My life-long labour now looks like a wish
To quench the burning bush I should have worshipped,
That fierce paradox beyond all natural Law.
It burns me now.

V

A weary busy-ness to find the truth: 220
And now I'm tired.
We have known resurrections. Lazarus I've met.
Others have heard of : not uncommon,
Nor the men interesting. Why Lazarus?
An insignificant young man with pious sisters,
The idle one inexplicably preferred.
It was dangerous to the nation and the Temple
To bring him back. The excited people
Might rise against the Occupying Power
And be massacred   230
By Pilate, as those others were whose blood
He mingled with their sacrifices, innocent as they.
Caiaphas was right. Order and Law
Must be preserved. Realism requires
We give in to superior force. No fate
Is worse than death. Insurrection
Is not our race's resurrection.
Is resurrection even desirable? A web of metaphor

Hangs round it; as grave-clothes on Lazarus   240
Baffled the body, so they my mind.
How should belief in anyone make life,
Anymore than a grown man can be reborn?
Metaphors are words, words fictions
That we must make to correspond with truth
And truth should make us free of words,
For truth is too complex for words.
A metaphor by nature is a lie.
Did he create a truth to match
A lie? How should truth 'live'?   250
When he promised that if one should
Keep his word, he never would see death,
The people hearing that took up great stones,
Thus to refute him. Things break words
As well as bones. Yet why feel such a need,
Such a promise to destroy? Do we love death
More than we know, are frightened by eternal life,
Angered by the call to another part
Of the mind, where truth looks like
Deceiving metaphor; preferring to keep,   260
Not a word, but ourselves for ourselves?
Preserving thus ourselves to death,
As I am dying now? He feared and hated death,
But then he died.

VI

Besides my failures (which now I have to accept)
Caused by lack of intelligence, errors,
Rash words, false assumptions, confusions,
Ill judgments, prejudices, sheer inattention,
Illicit, upsurging, distorted desires,
There is something that has always evaded me: 270
The key never grasped slipped through the grating,
The coin rolled into a dark corner,
The green pastures shaded in sunlight
With still waters, missed in the desert.
A child still cries some loss,
Locked in the dark cage of my old bones;
Perhaps I have tried too hard,
Misunderstood that desire, sense of desertion,
Hunger and thirst after the unconditioned
The arbitrary and so free, for the absurd   280
Happy ending of a conquered death,
For return to the Paradisal Garden,
Forgetting all good and evil, and only
Knowing the spring-time harvest of maintaining love.
There should have been some companion,
Some one to tell me something I cannot imagine.
Was it after all he whom I visited, whose words
My proud rationality rejected,
Mistaking the literal for primary sense,
Losing the sense in the meaning?   290

Have I been not foolish enough?
Failed in not failing enough?

For he surely succeeded in greatly failing.
Have I failed in succeeding at secondary things?

This also then must I accept,
Bitterest of all; such success as I have,
Neither to depreciate nor deprecate,
For it also was good in its kind.
And now there is failure, loss, and success,
And the greatest of these   300
Is not for me to determine.
I can accept, having nothing else to do
But hope for the best, emptied of pride and desire,
Dry bones left on the sand.

Can these bones live?

31–2	*Is. XXIV. 5 (RSV).*
100–4	*A characteristic maxim of the Talmud was 'Everyone is bound to teach with the exact words of the teacher'. EB, col. 4327.*
103–4	*Cf. John VII.14–5.*
116	*Cf. Matt. XXXIII.6.*
129	*Cf. John VII.52.*
145	*Cf. Henry Vaughan, 'The Night', 50.*
151	*Cf. Ps. XXXV.6 (PB).*
162	*Cf. Keats, 'Ode to a Grecian Urn', 49–50.*
174	*Cf. John VII.44.ff.*
177	*Cf. John XIX.39.*
214–5	*Primitive notions of a shadowy immortality, and of divine punishment, are here vaguely associated with the fires traditionally said to have been kept burning in the valley of*

Hinnom, and these in turn are associated with the splendour and fearfulness of God; cf. Ps. CXLIV.5 and Ps. CX.10.

228–37   Cf. *Luke XIII.1 and the dilemma of the Czechs from 20 August 1968 until the 'Velvet Revolution' of 1989.*

242   Cf. *John XI. 25.*

243   Cf. *John III.3-4.*

246   Cf. *John VIII.31-2.*

252–3   Cf. *John VIII.51–9.*

254   *When Boswell discussed with Johnson Berkeley's proof that matter is non-existent and everything in the universe 'ideal', and said that though we know it to be untrue yet it is impossible to refute, 'Johnson answered, striking his foot with mighty force against a large stone, till he rebounded from it – "I refute it thus".'* Boswell, Life of Johnson, *Year 1763.*

299-300   Cf. *I Cor. XIII.13.*

* 1969

SOLITUDES

SHE   – I am alone in a wide wide sea.
Who will speak to me? Where are you?
When will you come and speak? Speak.
Tell me what you mean. Tell.
Will you mean what you tell?

HE   – I sink in your lonely sea. Our hands
Will not meet. I drown. The fish suck my bones.
I rot in the depths of your sea.

OLD AGE

I

THE SEASON ADVANCES

Within the garden of my inner mind
I planted seeds that found the climate kind;
They have sprung up, but now the climate's cold.
The sun sinks down, the harvest's done. I'm old.

II

THE BONE-FIRE DIES DOWN

The fire in the blood may pale,
Bones snap and crumble, words only wail,
But the fire of the mind will live
Like a blue lambent flame above,
A crown of light on the dying fire;
Till it too consumes its own desire.

III

BORGES

An old man, a soft voice;
Shining eyes blinded
By the roaring fires
Of the abyss he looked into
Under the rocks,

The normal dark rocks
Of jobs and houses.
Now he sees only the fire,
Gropes his way,
Questions gently. Those eyes
Dissolve the stony
Darkness of our day,
To show the wonder beneath.
Was Homer like this?

THE TOWER

While looking for the city he found the forest.
Tracks led in several directions. Hesitating,
He took the second. Ancient nets but long grass
Recounted travellers before, not now.
The trees bowed over him, brambles clutched.
A stream tinkled somewhere. Darkness came
And no house in sight. His pack
Was heavy carrying his past life.
He could not chuck it.
He stumbled forward into an emptiness cleared
By earlier men who left a tower.
Behind him a silence concealed his pursuers.
What grisly beast, what violent man,
What malevolent ghost, what mindless horror
Might now assail? What hope of help
But in his own weakness, his own invisibility?
Run then, run as dizzying shades ensue.
The tower the only place, jagged under the sky.
What door was there, what unknown trap within?
Outside all stark in the moon. Enter,
Enter, since nothing in something is better
Than something in nothingness. What thick walls,
What stiff door. The thunder peals, a heavy threat.
A cloud comes over, down
The rain. Force the door, slam it
Behind. Safety. But no roof, only the
Criss-cross beams of fallen floors deflect

The envious sky, the rain. An impersonal enemy.
The pack must provide, tent, food,
A blanket of memories for warmth.
A temporary rest. Tomorrow a brighter day.

TROY SERIES

*The story of the siege and fall of Troy, consequent on Paris, son of king
Priam of Troy, seducing and running away with Helen, wife of the Greek
king Menelaus, echoes through European history from Homer to Chaucer
and Shakespeare, who use it as the backcloth for the love of Trojan Troilus
for the ultimately unfaithful Criseyde. Criseyde, daughter of Calcas the
soothsayer, who had gone over to the Greeks, was handed over to the
besieging Greeks in return for the Trojan Antenor, himself at last the
betrayer of Troy. This story of love and war is treated here as out of
historical time, part of the recurrent themes of war and betrayal in
modern as in ancient times, in a series of disparate comments, mingling
modern and ancient imagery of war.*

I

THE ONE ALONE

So curious that just one of many flowers,
Not the most rare nor brilliant, with sweetest scent,
Should be the one we want most deeply ours,
More inexpressibly than all be meant
(Though others might be plucked) to have such powers
That it uniquely from us must be rent.

II

IT IS THE CAUSE, IT IS THE CAUSE

Dogfights in the blue August sky
Helen watched from the walls, cheering them
To kill each other, for that lovely cause.
One plunged. Arose a column of black smoke;
A fly swatted by Zeus. Lovely Helen went to tea,
Inspiring glad young men with love, off-duty that day,
Who saw her, like death, only far away.

Dogfights: combats between fighter-planes.

III

LOVERS

They became lovers,
Or at least, she allowed him
To nuzzle her, rewarding
His devotion with stroking
And a friendly smile, finding
That the rhyme for adored
Is bored.
A master came by
Who called her to heel.
To love is to obey.
The other was left with the dreams
That make dogs whimper in sleep.

IV

TROILUS DESERTED

With you away the light drains from the sky.
All food has lost its taste, and meaningless
Is everything but war; where justified
I find, not sense, nor joy, nor light, but rage;
The reddened earth is dark with blood and groans.

V

A TROILUS-TYPE FOR ALL TIME

Sometimes they saw him coming back from battle,
Horse bloody, helmet battered, looking distantly
To where his heart lay with Criseyde: heartless
His fellow officers said, seeing him leap
Upon the trenches with his tommy-gun,
'A V.C. wallah' said the troops; they would prefer
To follow someone less devout and pure
Who knew when to take cover, not to push
Too hard; yet did not shoot him in the back,
Reflected glory gilding their own image
Of themselves, as cheering warmed the crowd.
He simplified their lives to all or nothing with
Inflexible pursuit of love and death,
Drawn always back to Troy to find his heart
With her from whom he lived and drank his happiness.
No drinking for him in the mess, ten gins
Before his lunch on days off-duty when

The tension must unstring or crack. Women
Or drink, they said, a man must have; and some
Tried both, telling their stories with the laughs
That recognise defeat, going in groups
To have their lives debriefed. ' —— *myself sober,*
And she hadn't touched my wallet'. '*Got a dose,*
But she was lovely'. '*Said she'd lost her husband'.*
Blind gropings seeking more than love and giving
Less. '*A little bastard's going to pop out soon,*
So that's one place I'm not going back to see'.
'*We'd spent our money all on drink. The Madam*
Wasn't pleased'.

                The lorries loaded men
At dawn who cursed or laughed, except for one,
Who screamed, being drunk: they caught and
    pitched him in
– He had his skinful punctured well by night –
But not so Troilus, whose drink was love.
He spilt no drop of it: they knew no woman
Of him: he could not kick his heart around
The market-place of common talk and sex.
No enemy could find it.
Criseyde kept it.
And then she threw it with the awkward gesture
    of a girl
Throwing a worthless ball: but it was packed like
    a grenade.
His rage and loss exploded on them all.
He lost his way: no soldier shot him. He was
Dead inside: his spirit lived in hell
And fierce Achilles only smashed a shell.

V.C. wallah. Second World War British army slang for those few exceptionally daring soldiers who were thought to be eager to earn the Victoria Cross, awarded only for supreme bravery and usually self-sacrifice in situations of extreme danger.

VI

PANDARUS CHASTE

Glad tutor of youth, Pandarus grew his grey hair long
Abandoned his tie (even a flowery one)
Encouraged the young to copulate – plenty of fish in
    that sea –
And while they fished read to himself an old
Romance but found no Galeotto there,
But had to seek his warmth from near the fire
Vicariously to satisfy desire.

The reference is to Chaucer's Troilus, Book III, 980 and more generally to Dante, Inferno V, known to Chaucer, which describes Paolo and Francesco in hell. They became lovers through reading together the love story of Lancelot and Guinivere, brought together by their friend Gallehault, in Italian Galeotto, also the name for a pimp. The book itself acts as a pimp, as does Pandar in Chaucer's story which gives his name in English to that function, deriving from Chaucer's poem.

VII

THERSITES

Sensual idealist, imprisoned
In a yapping dog, compulsive sniffer after
Genitalia; unable, for what he loved,
To mark it but by urination,
And barking at passers-by.

(This is Shakespeare's Thersites.)

VIII

CRISEYDE GOES TO THE GREEKS

She kissed them graciously – no wanton's touch.
Shakespeare got the story wrong. She wished to please,
She looked for comfort, peace, security,
For light and warmth, for colour, tenderness.
And like a tendril she must cling to what
Is nearest, strongest, even if more coarse.

IX

TROILUS DEAD

When I was alive I did not know,
When you were all I could or wished to know,
Entangled in the mighty tresses of your golden hair,

That I was blinded by a sun
That shone within my mind, not yours.
My love, you were my love.

If that was so, how I could I lose you then?
How could that sun go out, the darkness of a
    wintry day
Become my frozen life and anger, rage,
Cold Northern opposite of light, illuminated
Aurora Borealis, light the frozen waste of time
With no life-giving heat but lurid hate
Of all men, women too, but you?
My love, you were my life,
Till fierce Achilles hacked me down.
My life, you were my love.

X

AND LATER

She couldn't really understand why she
Should be blamed, though knowing that it would be so.
A realist like her father and her uncle –
Collaboration is what the world requires.
Why fight for what was doomed to fail; leave
Love in a garden which could never more
Be visited, its sanded alleys, grassy
Benches, running rank with weeds and unplucked flowers.
What purposes in life could so be served?
Much better to assume that Troilus too,
Shut out from joy, would look elsewhere,

When she half-willingly had gone to join
Her traitor-father on the winning side
And she among the Greeks with women few,
And Diomed was friendly, handsome, rich.
Why should the world call her alone a bitch?

The rumour she became a leper was
Untrue; Diómedes abandoned her.
But soft and friendly, tolerant of men
And women too, unable to say no,
With golden hair and wit and gaiety,
Her father learnéd, well-to-do, how could
She fail, respectful of all mastery,
To find a decent Greek prepared to love
Sufficiently to hold her, tell her what
To do, make all decisions, while he managed
His investments, and rose high within
The Grecian Civil Service? Years went by;
She bore three children and the golden hair
Faded to gray. Content to knit beside
The fire, yet still a gracious hostess with
A past that titillated old men's thoughts,
– Distinguished guests who called her 'my dear lady',
And hinted to their friends that once they'd known
Her rather well – she sometimes with a sigh
And smile indulged in thought the half-remembered past.
A comfortable world that made some sense;
Poor Troilus was always so intense.

XI

Remembrance

The sour smell of the smoking rubble passed;
The bones beneath the tumbled stones were softened.
The rain dispersed the brownness of the blood
And grass and willow-herb began to prise
Apart the locked allegiances of stone and lime
That mouldered on from all Troy's loyalties
Of man and woman, market-place and bed.
The level walks that thrilled with martial clank
And hasty hem and slipper; walls that boasted
Unconquered pride and views, protecting groves
Of ideal love; the towers that held the watchmen;
And the hovels of the poor who carried all this wealth
Upon their shoulders, oiled it with their sweat,
All, all were crumpled, lost, forgotten like
The boys who found the flighty Helen's face
A fair excuse to launch a thousand ships
And kill more thousands men and fight ten years,
Parents whose life departed with their sons,
The daughters raped, enslaved as washerwomen
Of a superior alien dirt. Where was their bravery
Then? Yet some crept back in winter to shelter
In muddy ruins, burn the last few sticks of Priam's
Altar for a cheering flame, and build a hovel
Where a palace stood. A little flame lives on.
Some folk survive in their diminished life
And poets later sing the glory and
The sadness of the past to give them hope,

That treachery may not always prevail,
That truth maintains its own validity,
And somewhere else new palaces are built.
Old lives and palaces are lost in silt.

ARTHURIAN NOTES

I

LANCELOT'S FIRST MEMORY

Dawn, a cold wind. Far off
The smouldering towers where I was born.
My mother wept, lost by the unknown lake
While I played with the pebbles on the shore;
They gleamed and flashed
Before they dried to dullness.
The sun was a great globe caught
Among the branches of the wintry trees.
And all now silent. No clash of swords
No screams and thuds, no roar of flames.
Suddenly, a woman stood beside us,
Unlike my mother, unbedraggled, smiling, beautiful.
I smell again her scented warmth.
I ran for comfort to her and she snatched me up
And sprang back in those nestling waters,
Down, down, in crystal depths,
Not cold nor warm, no smell of smoke or blood.
I grew up there; grew stronger than all men,
And courteous in that woman's world,
Was given intensest white to wear amongst
All flowering colours. And when I came to Arthur's court,
I saw it as a picture of the land I'd never left,
And knew that true when I saw Guinivere.

II

THE KNIGHT AND THE LADY

Desire for her totally filled him
And he was nothing to her, so he rode wildly away,
To carve out with his sword some deeds he could tell her,
To seek thus what he left behind, his bright armour
Slowly rusting, through winding forest paths,
And hardly noticed either primrose or falling leaf.
And when he met another obsessed solitary wanderer
Each set spear at the other, plunged spurs
Into the horse of his own desires,
Poured out his own blood to draw that of the other,
To transform the pain of his heart into another's
    broken bone.
And sometimes, exhausted by fighting, they found
They were brothers under the rusty armour of custom
    and self,
Destroying each other for a dream which they shared
But could never unite them. And his quest
Only ended by a dark lake into which
When he looked he saw neither his face nor the lady, and
He threw in not only his sword but his whole self.
The lady heard nothing of this, and was very content.

III

LANCELOT TO GUINEVERE

Your hair shines like gold, a light over the land.
Your face is a rose of freshness
Your scent sweeter than roses
Your voice is refreshing like the sound of a stream
                                    to a man dying of thirst.
O let my love be the wind that moves you.
You move like a young tree swept by the wind.

IV

PALOMIDES TO ISOLDE

These autumn birches, slender, tall make me
Envisage you. They sway without concern,
In graceful notice of the evening sun.
Green-gowned, they're touched with gold against the blue,
As if in thought apart, communing in
Themselves, until the storm lashes them into
Distress and wildness, and the sky rains tears.
And like you they are rooted firm elsewhere
In grounded love where I cannot approach.

Palomides, a brave Saracen knight, was hopelessly in love with Isolde, wife of King Mark, lover of Tristram.

V

TRISTRAM FIGHTING

And as I hacked I felt a sweet disturbance
Deep in my loins, not unlike childish thrills,
Not unlike when I loved Isolde before
I had her, a pleasure like a pain,
That made me grind my teeth and grin at blood
That spurted hotly on my hand from men
I never knew, and neither loved nor hated,
But into whose bodies, soft beneath the steel,
I drove with lovely crunch; and felt myself
Pure force, a lightning stroke, activity
Itself, discarnate unreflective appetite,
Devouring Death's devoted mindless maw.

VI

GAWAIN SPEAKS

You make too much of love you Lancelots
And Tristrams. Why should women bear the weight
Of such intensity? Is not your own
Enough for them? Such concentration makes
For tragedy. Exclusiveness is selfish,
Contrary to God's grace, which free and full
Will work promiscuously, embracing all
And firing with desire. Why restrain
Our overflowing love for beauty, goodness,
And not seek for welcome and a kiss

And more; but if they be not freely given
Go look elsewhere and not be sadly bound?
The forest's wide. Adventure calls us on.

VII

GAWAIN IS INTERVIEWED

*(The first line is a partial quotation from an interview given by Richard
Burton on BBC 1, 23 February 1983.)*

A great desire for women possessed me even
More than I possessed those women. Why
Should I hold back? They wanted me as much,
Or would they have agreed? What misery
Did I create that would not else have happened?
What children live, fathered unknown by me
Who would not lead a lesser life if sired
By some dull weak-balled hack?
You live a bored respected life; you give
No one unhappiness, nor any ecstasy;
Not brave enough to jettison when tired
Those girls, fear keeps you chaste and faithful while
You pine without the guts to win fresh nakedness,
Red newly eager lips, a brighter hair,
And now you rightly envy me, inventing
Compensatory Heaven and Hell. To make
Up for your lack of courage to enjoy yourself
And damn the consequences, you damn me.
I do not care, for I, like you, will be
Insentient through all the endless years,

Unthinking, unfeeling, non-existent self.
If you could now enjoy yourself you would
Be equal with me, who do not envy you.
Be reconciled with what you are, and let
Me be. Let appetite itself eat you,
Until devoured itself, still famished in its greed,
As still I lust and am not satisfied.

VIII

GAWAIN TO LANCELOT

You always have outshone me since you came
In your white armour to seduce the Queen,
And never have I understood you. Girls,
Or ladies rather, I have helped and won
In plenty, and my flush of life has played
A rosy part. I have not grudged you your
Obsessive secret passion known to all,
Superiority of one above the many,
Distrust it as I might. I have not grudged
The King's reliance on you more than me,
My youngest brother's loyalty to you
Above all other men. That you, that you
With your exalted heart and nobler ways,
Fastidious taste the best alone could please,
Should then kill Gareth, wildly striking one
        unarmed
While you fought king and kindred for her,
I never can forget, forgive. The wound
You later gave me as I struck at you

In necessary hate will never heal,
Be deeper in my brain, than this betrayal
For which I never rest nor seek a cure
Except the death of one or both of us.

Lancelot had inadvertently killed Gareth, Gawain's beloved younger brother, and Lancelot's most faithful friend, while fighting to rescue Guinivere from the punishment of adultery with him. But eventually Gawain, dying, did forgive Lancelot.

IX

LANCELOT'S MADNESS

The black river flooded the meadow which I thought
At last was mine, to pick the finest flower.
Instead of what I thought it was, a sea
Of mud arose around me. I sprang shrieking,
Half choked with noisome sludge, gasping for air,
I tore off all my clothes and ran among
The brambles that would tear from me the stain.
The forest only with its darkness held
Not comfort nor redemption but refuge.
How could I bear that men should see my state?
The mud had burnt me. Ineluctable
Desire of sweetness, bright and warm
Had of itself it seemed welled up, in filth,
Disloyal and untrue; blind and mad.
But now all things seem necessary; the pain
And dirt, betrayal, loss, were in themselves

The fertile bed in which I laid the seed
That only there could flower as Galahad.

*When Lancelot found he had been tricked by Elaine into sleeping with her
he ran mad in the forests.*

X

Guinevere

The river of my own life bore me on
As if my conscious self were but a bright
Uncertain ship upon the darker stream,
With velvet sails and silken cabins and
An iron keel, but rudderless, no one
To steer; like and unlike that other ship
Which bore the jewelled unrotting lovely corpse
Of Perceval's chaste sister, where Lancelot
With Galahad, upon that fatal Quest
Which foolish youthful longing for ideal
And absolute truth had wantonly provoked,
Involuntary father with his son,
– Why could he not have been begot on me? –
Together let themselves be carried as
The sport of tides and wills beyond themselves.
My ship is not less fine than Blancheflur's was.
I am no corpse, and Lancelot would play
Upon me to our joy as Arthur had,
Until the cares and griefs of government
Caused him less care and greater grief for me.

My ship, my self, was not my own. My true
And deeper self lay in the surging current
Now dark, now bright, tumultuous or calm.
Two men alone were good enough to board
My sides. I welcomed each, and surely there
Was room enough for both, although I was
But one, of beauty that transfixed men's minds.
My current flowed past sunlit flowers and woods,
Through gorges by dark cliffs of barren death.
I could not choose, no more than they could hold
Themselves from the enchantment of my glance.
Nor could the waterfall's approaching roar
Be other than the necessary end.

*Though Lancelot was in intention faithful to Guinivere he was tricked
by Elaine into begetting his son Galahad, the purest of knights, on
her. Blancheflur was Percival's sister. The Quest was that for the
Holy Grail.*

XI

ABOUT GUINEVERE

What held them? So many men, so different,
The king, his courtiers, steel-headed warriors,
Above all, Lancelot, whose bright armour glowed
From inner fire repelling cold steel's harm.
And she, a queen; no mother, save to those
Who worshipped her; still childish, needing guard;
A flower, a flame, not living to herself,

White fantom, most alive when held within
Those longing minds that struck each other dead.

The Welsh original of the name Guinivere means 'white fantom'.

XII

MERLIN TO NINIVE

'And he was assoted uppon her' (Malory)

How very peculiar to feel
About you as I do, since
You grant me no feeling.
People in my position
Should not be so soft
Towards such softness as yours.
If I were harder you might be
Tougher but easier.
Of course you're so nice,
And beautiful, and discreet as I trust,
And joyous (much of the time)
And thin, and sweet-smelling.
How should I not be softened?
But it's peculiar to feel
That the world's a bit different
When you're here;
While you have a barrier
Of nothingness around you
That prevents you feeling.
Unlike the world, you are indifferent.

And thus you have knowledge of me
And I know nothing (really) of you.
And that nothing hides something,
While a nothingness, wanting something, is in me.

Merlin was the wizard who managed Arthur's birth and tried to guide him. As an old man he fell in love with the young Ninive.

XIII

NINIVE SPEAKS

What can you give me that I cannot get from others?
I need no father and I want a lover.
Let him be sappy, young, resilient, smooth
And full of fun and laughter, giving me sons
And daughters, for I know the forms of life
And only lack the substance and the wealth.

XIV

MERLIN TO NINIVE

You have an independent inner light
Which shines through flesh, both yours and mine,
To penetrate the darkness of my soul.
What is it that I see? Do I see you
Or some reflection of transcendent fire?
Yet you it must be, for no other woman
Have I known, though still I do not yet know you,

Virginity the price I paid for power,
For knowledge. I did not gain or learn what Arthur,
Lancelot, Tristram, ignorant men if noble,
Knew from their raging blood, and won in love.
No children have I, not a lover, nor
Any hope of gain save you alone:
And only you will fill the cup which love,
Not learning, power, will fill with living light.

XV

NINIVE TO MERLIN

You have a hoary head if yet the rest
Is green. I see you, imaging all wisdom
And power, which I too want and need.
You paid the price. I will not do the same.
What force compels you on me but your same
Remorseless drive to conquer life; first power
Through knowledge, and then strength from me?
I see though dimly in the darker places
Of your mind. I do not need the warmth of your
Embrace, nor care about your dark but
Human longing which a younger man
Might have, and please me with more handsome face.
I want the treasure of your knowledge, power
Which lies within that chamber brightly lit
And ordered with calm rationality
Which can command, or if it will, destroy the world.

XVI

Merlin's youthful desire

One should not pay too much attention, I thought
To one's feelings. I thought. Lost in thought, as I thought,
I was lost in the dark wood of desire
To know, cutting down and chopping up
The Tree of Knowledge into convenient lengths,
As pitprops for the mining of depths of further desire
To penetrate the secrets of the world and of hearts,
From there to arise at unexpected moments
To control. Fate could not be commanded
But might be managed as I managed myself,
Or as I now know, my desire managed me.
And so I had my desire, to be strong and alone,
To know so much except myself, for I thought
That later would be time for love, and so
There was, and I loved, later, but too late,
And the secret tunnels collapsed, the wood ran wild,
And I burnt on the pyre of dried out timber.

XVII

Merlin and the Grail

My love unsatisfied burns up myself:
The fire that could warm others cinders me
To cold and colourless an inward life.
The plenitude and light I never sought
Which might come from the Grail, for I saw

That just as evil in its purest form
Could blast the garden of this world and bring
In death and sorrow, so goodness at its height
Was equally destructive of the humble
Cobbling up of human struggle to make do,
The compromises, practical devices,
Shifts and stratagems and management
We need to make a tolerable life, if not the best,
Of where we find ourselves, poor fallible
But not entirely worthless children, men and women.
Nor did I look for power, only influence.
And wife and child I left aside to seek
Some knowledge how to guide contentious men and kings.
One should not pay too much attention to
One's personal desires. And now I lose
Direction dazzled by a foolish girl
Who will betray me, locked up in
The darkness of my barren inner mind.

XVIII

MERLIN ENTOMBED

No more. You walk away and take the light
Out of my mind for ever. Empty and black.
My mind a wiped-out slate, those agéd clichés
Of youth, of beauty, fallen to chalk-dust.
The emptiness contains all of your image,
Reflecting now the equal blankness of
The image that you never held of me;
Two black and empty mirrors replicate

The infinite non-being of illusion,
Which now illuminates itself as truth,
Where absence testifies validity.
Nothing comes to nothing; a bitter taste
Itself deludes by witnessing delusion.
The darkness of oblivion now is truth.

XIX

MERLIN FROM PRISON IN WHICH HE HAS ALLOWED NINIVE TO ENTOMB HIM FORESEES THE DEATH OF ARTHUR

In darkness, sonless myself, dazzled by
Another's beauty I foresee how he
Could only seek the bright ghost leading to
The ultimate loss. How could he forego
That transcendent image? And I who had
Procured his mother, watched his childhood, more
Than parent, must endure the loss before
It happens, seeking a mother younger than
Himself to keep alive my hope of seeding.
Seed yet unsown from me is sown and blown.
No scattered progeny will fertilise the world,
Though images of beauty, courage, loss and joy
Will sound from out the beating of my heart,
Notes richly roused upon an empty drum.

'Bright ghost'; Guinivere. See above, p 231.

XX

GRAIL-GRACE

ARTHUR: I see that wanting it I did not welcome.
Repletion sickens; appetite is dead.
For many years I held together a fractious crowd
Of emulous proud touchy men, not all as brave
As they would have me think, not chaste
    for certain,
In faith careless, or dependent on the rest, or me,
But having some desire for goodness, hope,
For friends, for deep-set satisfactions found
In fire-lit groups of men who risked their lives
Together, sometimes helped or saved each other,
And who could say 'we saved the kingdom' or
'The lady' 'on such a day', 'against such odds'
And thereby think themselves as 'big', and part
Of something bigger. That larger self
Was my ideal, the Court, the Table Round,
A present unity of various men
Linked in a loyal brotherhood. But yet
The last most perilous seat remained unfilled,
A flaw, a hope, to show something must still
Be done, or come; a mystery to me,
A promise from a realm which no-one knew,
Beyond control, that sent a grace, a threat.
And who should take that seat must be unknown,
Perfection marking him, whose right it was
To occupy it as his own – not mine.
I knew that if I ever might achieve

The kingdom, my kingdom, as I wished,
Peaceful, fruitful, just, and beautiful,
He must come. But I did not seek extremes.
A reasonable, good, pragmatic sense
(Accepting casualties in battle, errors
In us all, including me) I thought
Was all that could, or should, be hoped.
The truth is different. To get the better,
You have to seek the best, uncomfortable,
Unaccommodating and disruptive,
Which destroys the engendering good,
Just as the bad may rend its origins.
So at the end, hope is fulfilled, and faith
No longer needed: love and death are one.

LANCELOT: The Pentecostal feast that year retained
Its comfortable sense of cyclic hope
That faith would not too soon be justified,
And reigning love retain its single aim.
But all being gathered in the hall the dark
Suddenly closed in – clash of shutters,
     candles out.
The boy walked in, my son, the unwilled bastard,
Got by persistent wish upon an image
I rejected of the true infertile
Guinivere. He imaged and transcended
Me in turn; divine deceit more true,
More confident, more gentle, more dismaying.
He took no note of me or of the King,
Who stared, leaning on his chair's back, till all
Was lost in blackness, save the boy, who took

The seat that, perilous, never had been filled.
Great silence struck those cheerful oafs,
     my friends,
A fear of new dimensions in the world
Appearing, which we had relied upon,
But to which logic then would nail our limbs
More stretched than in the bed of human love,
More pained than when in joust or tournament
The spear of hate had pierced our iron sides.
Within the dark new light began to live,
Unlike the warm accustomed flickering flame
Of fire and candle-light, the silver gleam;
New light, internal, unórigined, not cold,
Not human, yet still as if each one of us,
In all our imperfections gave out some
Of it, and yet we looked beyond. We heard
A music that in plangency transfused
The mind. It was as if we were and were
Not those who saw and heard, and what
Was seen and heard – the bloody lance
That dripped into that bowl, the Grail,
Which held all love and suffering as a drink.
It was not in itself, but gave to us,
What we both had and wanted, while the boy,
Impassive, watched it as the destiny
That he had brought but now must further seek.
That was the climax of our days. I felt
No pride in Galahad, or in myself
But felt again the old desire transformed
To serve and follow free, to hold and not
Possess.

I looked at Arthur and the Queen.
In both was pain. She, childless, beautiful,
Looked long at Galahad, reflection of
Her vacancy. But Arthur, who had got
His only son, incestuous bastard, filial
Parody, looked only at the Grail,
The long-sought grace, tears falling on his
    grizzled beard.

GUINIVERE: That cold pure boy brings warmth and light
    and food:
At what a price. Give me my Lancelot,
Mine alone. Promiscuous love will not
Assuage my need, lighten my day, fill up
My emptiness.

THE QUEST

(i)

Though all must go, they do not know what way,
Nor what they seek and most will soon give up,
Return to find normality, yet change
Has happened. We cannot now go back
To find what once we were. Nothing is the same.

(ii)

The pallor of the wet and windy sky
At evening, underlined by the black wood,
Marks out the ruined tower, the leaden lake.

The harness jingles: smell of leather and horse-sweat,
The rotting smell of corpses. Where to sleep tonight?

(iii)

O Carbonek! O distant land! Where love
And death shine out as one, and only Bors
The ordinary man, who cannot see
The brightness, will bring the tale of it back home.

*The poem refers to the annual gathering of King Arthur's court at
Pentecost, when all the knights renewed their vows. Lancelot had been
tricked by magic in the past to beget Galahad on Elaine, believing her to be
Guinivere. Galahad appeared at the Pentecostal Feast and he alone could
occupy the Siege Perilous, the last of the seats of the Round Table. At his
first appearance the Grail also appeared for a moment, as described. All
the knights set off in quest of it. Only Galahad, Percival and Bors came to
the castle of Carbonek where it was found. Galahad and Percival
remained and died at Carbonek. Bors returned. The Grail was thought to
be the vessel that received the blood and water shed from the side of Christ
on the Cross. The Maimed King is he whose wound caused his kingdom to
lie waste, and was cured by Galahad. Arthur's son was Mordred, the
bastard he begot on Morgause, not knowing her at that time to be his half
sister. In the end Mordred rebelled against Arthur and in a final battle
they killed each other.*

XXI

The Hermit

*The Hermit, once a knight of the Round Table, takes
in the wounded Lancelot*

I once made wounds: and now I bind them up,
A practice equally in vain. This Lancelot
Will return to love and battle, synonyms
For death, to which I also move at slower pace.
I left behind first, sex; wine lasted longer,
But I have drunk it to the bitter dregs.
Religion now remains, the ragged tatters
Stained with blood, and brains, my own and others,
To use for bandages; ashamed of them
When they were splendid, so neglected; now
There's nothing else, and I'm ashamed that I'm
Ashamed they're now so poor. I will wash them,
Not with my tears, the maudlin tears of age,
But with the practice of a washerwoman
And nurse; useful now though useless in the end.
I loved a lady once and knew her well;
Exclusive singularity, but now
Such union's gone. I seek promiscuous grace,
That goes beyond the loyalty to one,
Not seeking lovely lips and limbs which drive
A man to hungry madness. My need is
Not to mingle flesh, be torn with brambles of desire,
But freedom from the rusty chains of lust.

Alone, I seek the meeting-place of all;
My pain the only road to find the love
Which heals the wounds of living death; in thought,
Which will not solve the puzzle of the world
But go beyond it; hoping for what we,
Believing in validity of pain
In faith as much without a proof as all
The other underlying modes of being
Of knight, of merchant, ploughman, scholar, priest.
I will to not-will; know to not-know; see
Only a nothingness; plunge or rise up
Beyond what's good or bad. I'll watch and pray,
And bind meanwhile the everbleeding wounds,
Until peace passing understanding comes.

XXII

ARTHUR BROODS BEFORE THE LAST BATTLE

Where are you, Guinivere, Morgause and Lancelot?
What should I differently have done?
Why should I alone when young not have
A woman – and I did not know Morgause
To be my sister. When all the court knew love,
And not one woman chaste, as testing showed,
And kings have right to all, should I refrain?
And then with Mordred's birth, I killed all those
About that age, in order to preserve
The greater good of courtly life and land.
The wails of mourning mothers haunt the wind
That now assaults my face. And when I married

Guinivere, though told the future clear enough
No telling could deny the racing blood
Her beauty spurred in me with sweetest pain
And Lancelot was not there, my wished-for son.

XXIII

Work and sleep

'I am slothful in the mornings'
Said young Arthur,
'But there is much to be done.
In the grave is enough of sleeping'.

'Sleep is hard to get',
Said old Merlin:
'Time spent sleeping is rarely wasted'.

So in the end both were satisfied.
Stone blanketted their graves.

l. 4 is a quotation from some Elizabethan worthy.

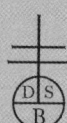

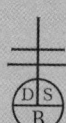